# SPEAKING
# for Academic Purposes

## Introduction to EAP

**Robyn Brinks Lockwood**

Stanford University

**Keith S. Folse**

University of Central Florida

**Series Editor: Keith S. Folse**

University of Michigan Press
Ann Arbor

Copyright © by the University of Michigan 2017
All rights reserved
Published in the United States of America
The University of Michigan Press
Printed and bound by CPI Group (UK) Ltd, Croydon, CR0 4YY

∞ Printed on acid-free paper

ISBN-13: 978-0-472-03670-7

2020    2019    2018    2017                4        3        2        1

# Acknowledgments

Robyn would like to thank Keith Folse, her co-author and series editor, for his valuable feedback and input, and Kelly Sippell, for her constant support and dedication to producing strong English language materials. Personal thanks to the original Brinks clan, Virgil, June, and Tim, and the next generation, Darrin and Nathan, for being as proud of me as I am of all of them. And, to my husband, John, for continually giving me all open desk, table, and floor space for my page proofs.

The publisher, series editor, and authors would like to thank the educational professionals whose reviews helped shape the Four Point series, particularly those from these institutions: Auburn University, Boston University CELOP, Central Piedmont Community College, Colorado State University, Daytona Beach Community College, Duke University, Durham Technical College, Georgia State University, Harding University, Hillsborough Community College, Northern Virginia Community College–Alexandria Campus, Oregon State University, University of California–San Diego, University of Nevada at Las Vegas, University of North Carolina–Charlotte, and Valencia Community College.

*Grateful acknowledgment is made to the following authors, publishers, and individuals for permission to reprint copyrighted or previously published materials.*

Library of Congress for photos of John F. Kennedy and Richard M. Nixon.

Thinkstock.com for all other photos.

*Every effort has been made to contact the copyright holders for permission to reprint borrowed material. We regret any oversights that may have occurred and will rectify them in future printings of this book.*

The University of Michigan Press thanks: Anna Dean, Kelsey Dean, Angie Feak, Scott Ham, Adam Jazairi, Sheryl Leicher, Karen Pitton, and Serena Wu for contributing their talent to the videos.

# 4 Point Overview

The **4 Point** series is designed for English language learners whose primary goal is to succeed in an academic setting. While grammar points and learning strategies are certainly important, academic English learners need skills-based books that focus on reading, listening, and speaking, as well as the two primary language bases of vocabulary and grammar.

The Introduction to EAP level is designed for students in academic programs who need a more general introduction to authentic academic content. The discrete skills **4 Point** volumes are designed for programs and courses that want a more intensive focus on authentic academic content in one skill area. We have created these volumes on individual skills because customers wanted authentic academic content for this level, but they wanted to be able to focus on one skill at a time. The ultimate goal is to help your students improve these skills and earn a **4.0** (G.P.A.).

**4 Point** covers academic skills while providing reinforcement and systematic recycling of key vocabulary issues and further exposure to grammar issues. The goal of this series is to help students improve their ability in each of these critical skills and thereby enable the students to have sufficient English to succeed in their final academic setting, whether it be community college, college, or university.

Many ESL students report great difficulties upon entering their academic courses after they leave the safe haven of their English class with other non-native speakers and their sympathetic and caring ESL teachers. Their academic instructors speak quickly, give long reading assignments due the next day, and deliver classroom lectures and interactions at rapid, native speed. In sum, ESL students who have gone through a sheltered classroom setting are in for a rather rude awakening in a new learning situation where English is taken for granted and no one seems to understand or care much about the new reality of the dilemmas facing ESL students. Through these materials, we hope to lessen the shock of such an awakening. The activities in **4 Point** achieve the goal of helping students experience what life beyond the ESL classroom is like while they are still in a sheltered classroom.

These volumes focus very heavily on vocabulary because language learners know that they are way behind their native-speaker counterparts when it comes to vocabulary. Each book highlights key vocabulary items, including individual words, compound words, phrasal verbs, short phrases, idioms, metaphors, collocations, and longer set lexical phrases. In learning vocabulary, the two most important features are frequency of retrievals (i.e., in exercises) and the spacing between these retrievals. Interactive web-based exercises provide additional opportunities for students to practice their academic vocabulary learning at their convenience (**www.press.umich.edu/elt/compsite/4Point/**).

## Using the Exercises in This Book (Speaking)

The exercises accompanying the passages are meant to strengthen a range of speaking skills, notably:

- understanding classroom discourse
- using academic language functions
- recognizing signal words and phrases
- developing vocabulary
- synthesizing information

In addition to more general speaking tasks, most units include a specific speaking focus, such as making presentations and participating in group discussions. Six video clips can be found online at **www.press.umich.edu/elt/compsite/4Point/**.

### Pre-Speaking Activities

A range of pre-speaking questions is included; each has the purpose of activating prior knowledge about and generating interest in the topics in the unit. Often these questions provide opportunities for students to anticipate content and, therefore, may be revisited throughout the unit. All of the pre-speaking tasks lead to pair or small group discussions.

### In-Class and Out-of-Class Interactions/Classroom Discourse

Each unit includes activities based on the in-class interactions students are likely to encounter in post-secondary classrooms. Throughout the units, students participate in group activities that allow them to use the speaking phrases taught in the unit. Other activities include information gaps, rankings, and in-depth discussions. Each unit contains a Making Contact activity designed to put students into interactive situations with native speakers and to research phrases used in their discipline.

In addition, the video includes several features of everyday language that are designed to help make the video more realistic for students. For example, the interactions include some false starts, error corrections, and reductions. Also, in the attempt to help students understand more than professional native speakers, the online videos features fluent non-native speakers to replicate university settings.

Six video clips are provided on the companion website (www.press.umich. edu/elt/compsite/4Point/) to analyze for language, tone, and nonverbal cues as well as to generate discussion on academic tasks. Throughout the interaction, the students use many of the phrases and employ the strategies taught in the unit—and, in some cases, not using the best communication strategies. ELLs will have the opportunity to hear the phrases used in a natural conversation, practice their listening skills, analyze verbal and nonverbal communication skills of the students, and think critically about and discuss the interaction with their classmates. Questions in the book require students to listen for certain phrases and identify what they mean; to notice the tone of voice and think about how it changes the dynamics of a discussion; to recognize the influence of nonverbal communication by increasing their awareness of facial expressions, gestures, and other cues; and compile all of these ideas into an analytical discussion about the interaction in the video.

## Synthesizing: Projects and Presentations

The summative task for each unit includes four projects that relate to the topic and encourage practice of the concepts. Students prepare projects and presentations based on what they have learned via the readings, discussions, or online or library research. For group projects, students should be given adequate time to clarify group roles and to work on their projects.

## Rapid Vocabulary Review and Vocabulary Log

A vocabulary review task appears at the end of each unit and gives students another opportunity to check their understanding of key words. The correct answer is a synonym or brief definition. Crucial to the vocabulary acquisition process is the initial noticing of unknown vocabulary. ELLs must notice the vocabulary in some way, and this noticing then triggers awareness of the item and draws the learner's attention to the word in all subsequent encounters, whether the word is read in an activity or heard in a conversation. To facilitate noticing and multiple retrievals of new vocabulary, we have included a chart listing 15 key vocabulary items at the end of each unit. This Vocabulary Log has three columns and requires students to provide a definition or translation in the second column and then an original example or note about usage in the third column. As demonstrated in *Vocabulary Myths* (Folse 2004, University of Michigan Press), there is no research showing that a definition is better than a translation or vice-versa, so we suggest that you let ELLs decide which one they prefer. After all, this log is each student's individual vocabulary notebook, so students should use whatever information is helpful to them and that will help them remember and use the vocabulary item. If the log information is not deemed useful, the learner will not review this material—which defeats the whole purpose of keeping the notebook. In the third column, students can use the word in a phrase or sentence, or they can also add usage information about the word such as *usually negative, very formal sounding,* or *used only with the word* launch. To encourage use of the Vocabulary Log, 10 extra lines are provided so that students can choose their own vocabulary items.

# Contents

# 1 Architecture: Applied Science

An applied science is one in which people use science to do something practical. Architecture is often considered an applied science because it involves using science to construct something that people use, such as buildings. Architects must think about design so the building looks nice, while also considering technical aspects to make the building safe and functional. This unit explores architecture as an art and as a science.

## Part 1: Architecture as an Art and a Science

### Pre-Speaking Activities

Writing a definition for the word *architecture* can be difficult because it involves both art (or design) and science (or engineering). Some architects like the blend because they have a chance to be both creative and practical. Even for the earliest works of architecture, the blend of art and science was a part of the field. Answer these questions with a partner.

1. How do you think architecture is like an art? Like a science? Explain your reasons.

   _____

   _____

   _____

2. What types of structures would you want to develop? Buildings, bridges, or some other structure? Why?

   _____

   _____

   _____

3. What kinds of things do you think an architect needs to think about when planning a new structure?

   _____

   _____

   _____

# Strategy: Encouraging Discussion

In English, it is important to notice when a speaker or leader is encouraging you to participate. There are several strategies a speaker may use to ask you to participate. These strategies are good to use when you are the speaker, too.

## Ask Questions

- when you can't hear the speaker

  Sorry. I couldn't hear what you said about that building. Will you say it again?

- when you can't understand the content

  Excuse me. I don't know what kind of architecture that is. Can you explain it?

- when you want to make sure you understood (especially with names and numbers)

  When did you say that happened? 1988?

- when you need more information

  I have not heard of that architect. How do you spell that name?

- when you want more or extra information

  Where is that building?

## Make Requests

- for more information

  That type of architecture is new for me. It's interesting. I'd like to learn more.

- for something to be repeated

  Would you repeat the question, please?

  Will you say that again?

- for an example

  What is an example?

*Paraphrase*

- when you want to make sure you understand

  So he's excluding bridges as a work of art, right?

  Did you say _____?

  When you said . . . , did you mean that . . . ?

*Use Voice Fillers*

| | | |
|---|---|---|
| Hmmm. | Go on. | Right. |
| Oh. | Yes. Yeah. | Really? |
| Wow. | Uh huh (positive). | Tell me more. |
| That's interesting. | Unh uh (negative). | Cool/That's cool. |

### Pronunciation Note

**Intonation** is the pitch—or the rising and falling of the voice when someone is speaking. In English, sometimes a person's pitch goes up. Other times, a person's pitch falls. When asking questions that that have a yes or no answer, use **rising** intonation. When asking *wh-* questions, use **falling** intonation. If you use the opposite intonation, the speaker might think you are being rude, misunderstanding the information, or expressing a different emotion.

| Yes-No Questions | Wh- Questions |
|---|---|
| Do you live near here? | Where do you live? |
| Is tomorrow's test on both chapters? | What is tomorrow's test on? |
| Have you visited the Eiffel Tower? | Which famous sites have you visited? |

### Pronunciation Note

Some voice fillers can use rising intonation as well, making them sound like a question and encouraging the speaker to repeat or give more information; such as *Tell me more* or *Oh*. Review the list of fillers given.

## Encouraging Discussion

Work in groups of four. Choose a paragraph from a textbook or an article from a newspaper (campus, local, or national). Imagine you are leading a discussion on the topic with other students. Read the paragraph or article you selected aloud to the other members of your group. Be prepared for them to encourage discussion by using the strategies in the box on pages 3–4. Take turns being the group leader and a participant. Use this space to take notes while your classmates are leading.

Leader 1

_____

_____

_____

_____

_____

Leader 2

_____

_____

_____

_____

_____

Leader 3

_____

_____

_____

_____

_____

# Speaking

## Greetings

Before starting a conversation or discussion, most people begin with a greeting. This sometimes breaks the ice and helps the interaction seem friendly and open. There are many greetings in English, and some are more formal than others.

| Formal | Informal |
|---|---|
| Hello. | Hi. |
| Good morning/afternoon/evening. | Hey. |
| How are you? | How you doing? |
| It's nice to see you. | What's up? |
| It's been a long time. | Long time, no see. |
| How have you been? | How's it going? |
| How are things going? | What's new? |

## Using Greetings

Think about greetings, and answer these questions with a partner. Then share your ideas with the class.

1. Would you greet each of these people formally or informally?

    a. your English teacher _____

    b. an instructor in your department _____

    c. the department chairperson _____

    d. your roommate _____

    e. a relative _____

    f. a cashier at the bookstore _____

    g. a new classmate who sits next to you in class _____

2. What greetings do you frequently use every day? Add other greetings to the list on page 6.

_____

_____

3. What things affect the greeting and/or the response? Does the place or time of the interaction matter? Does the formality of the greeting affect the response?

_____

_____

## Making Contact

Choose three greetings from the list on page 6, and greet three different English speakers. Take notes on the greeting you used, the response you received, and the details of the interaction (person's status, age, and gender, the time of day, and the location). Follow the example. Be prepared to discuss your data with the class.

| Your Greeting | The Person's Response | Details of the Interaction |
|---|---|---|
| Hi. | Hi. | classmates, same age, male, morning, hallway |
| | | |
| | | |
| | | |

## Part 2: Architecture as an Art

### Pre-Speaking Activities

What do you know about architecture? Although schools and universities offer classes about architecture, most people do not know much about it. They do not realize the science and engineering that goes into making a building. However, many buildings are recognizable and remembered for their unique appearance. The design is the creative side of architecture. Answer these questions with a partner.

1. Do you recognize these places? What are they? What city or country are they in?

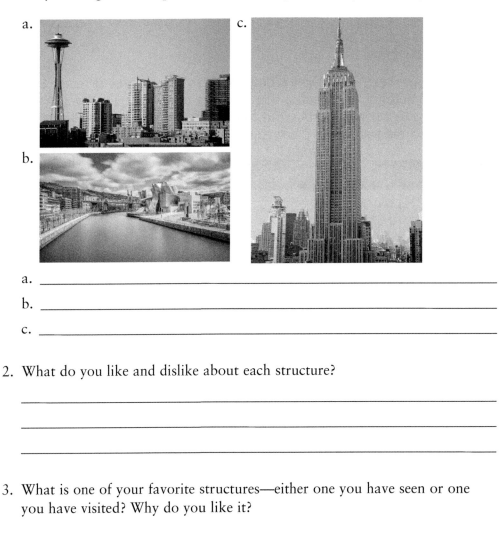

a. _____

b. _____

c. _____

2. What do you like and dislike about each structure?

_____

_____

_____

3. What is one of your favorite structures—either one you have seen or one you have visited? Why do you like it?

_____

_____

## Strategy: Expressing Your Feelings

In English, speakers use different ways to express their feelings.

*Language*

Sometimes you can tell how someone feels by the words they choose to use or by extra words they add before a descriptive word.

I'm <u>so</u> happy we got to see the Sydney Opera House.

The Guggenheim Museum is <u>incredibly</u> beautiful.

The airport was <u>huge</u>!

*Tone*

You can also tell how a person feels by the particular tone of voice he or she uses. A person can sound happy, confused, or upset, or they can convey any other emotion.

*Nonverbal Communication*

Sometimes speakers convey feelings without saying anything at all.

- **Facial expressions** (smiling, frowning, open or closed eyes, open or closed mouth, raised eyebrows)
- **Eye contact** (direct or indirect)
- **Posture** (leaning forward, sliding down in the chair, standing or sitting straight)
- **Head movement** (nodding, shaking, tipping)
- **Gestures** (hand movements, symbols)

Notice how many speakers combine language, tone, and nonverbal communication to make their communication more powerful. Recognizing these things will help you understand others and help you better convey how you feel.

### Pronunciation Note

**Tone** can also be conveyed through emphasis.

I simply <u>can-NOT</u> understand what that architect was thinking. (emphasize certain words)

I just <u>lo-ooove</u> the design of the Beijing National Stadium. (longer vowel)

The airport was <u>so-ooo</u> big that it was **very** overwhelming. (longer vowel)

## Listening for and Expressing Feelings

Write three sentences about buildings you can think of or are familiar with. Say them to a partner, expressing yourself clearly in English. Use a strategy or combination of strategies from the box on page 9. Can your partner tell how you feel about the structures?

Your Sentences

_____

_____

_____

# Speaking

### I'm Sorry and Excuse Me

Two common phrases in English are *I'm sorry* and *Excuse me*. They are used often but for different reasons. Recognizing the differences will help you understand what other people mean and will make your own purpose clear when you are the speaker.

| USE *I'm sorry* TO . . . |
| --- |
| apologize for forgetting or not knowing a person's name |
| apologize for hurting a person's feelings |
| apologize for interrupting |
| ask for repetition |
| correct something said incorrectly |
| express sadness for hurting a person physically |
| express sympathy for someone's situation |
| regret being late, saying the wrong thing, or losing something |
| show you are sincere and accept responsibility for your actions |
| turn down an invitation |

| USE *Excuse me* TO . . . |
| --- |
| ask someone for a favor |
| be formal in academic or professional places |
| be polite after coughing, clearing your throat, or sneezing, etc. |
| be polite with people you do not know well |
| get someone's attention |
| interrupt a speaker nicely |
| leave a room, conversation, or group, etc. |

## Analyzing the Situation

Work with a partner. For each situation, decide what you would say or do. Include **I'm sorry** or **Excuse me**. Choose two situations, and then write a dialogue for each on a separate sheet of paper. Try to extend the conversation after the **I'm sorry** or **Excuse me**.

1. You're at the library and you need to know what time it is so you won't miss your architecture class. You want to ask the student sitting at the next table.
   _____

2. The teacher is collecting the design homework assignment, but you are not finished with it. You want to explain to the teacher. _____
   _____

3. Your pen ran out of ink during an office hour with your English teacher. You need to borrow a pen to finish taking notes about the advice for your building design. _____

4. You're at a party talking with a friend when you see a classmate from your architecture class come into the room. You want to go say hello. _____
   _____

5. You are unable to attend a party for your friend who won the school's design contest. You need to tell your friend you will not be there. _____
   _____

6. You dropped water on your roommate's model building. You want to tell your roommate what happened. _____

# Video: Managing Group Dynamics

Listen to the students work together to decide on the type of building to report on for their architecture class. Discuss the questions in a small group.

## Focus on Language

1. What greetings do the students use? Refer to those given on page 6.

   _____

   _____

2. What can you guess about their relationships based on their greetings?

   _____

   _____

3. Make a list of when you hear the phrases *I'm sorry* and *Excuse me*. What does each one mean? Do you think there are other times students could use the phrases?

   _____

   _____

   _____

4. Write any phrases or idioms that you are not familiar with. Discuss what they mean and in what type of interactions they are appropriate.

   _____

   _____

## Focus on Tone

1. Describe the tone and emotion used by each member of the group.

   _____

   _____

2. How can you tell how each person is feeling?

_____

_____

3. Is each person's tone appropriate for the situation? Why or why not?

_____

_____

## Focus on Nonverbal Communication

1. What nonverbal cues are used to show how each member of the group feels about ideas from other group members?

_____

_____

2. Were any of these inappropriate? Why or why not?

_____

_____

3. Which student do you think is the best at nonverbal communication? Is this good or bad for the interaction?

_____

_____

_____

## Summary

1. What strategies do the students use to encourage communication? Refer to the box on pages 3 and 4.

_____

_____

_____

_____

2. Which student uses the best combination of words, tone, and nonverbal communication? Support your answer.

_____

_____

_____

_____

3. Who would you most want to work with? Why? Who would you rather not work with? Why?

_____

_____

_____

_____

### Information Gap

One interesting feature of architectural design is a structure's length—how long it is. This is especially true about bridges. Designs may vary based on the kind of traffic that the bridge carries.

Work with a partner to complete the chart. Person A has Chart 1 on page 15 and Person B has Chart 2 on page 16. Work back to back to complete the information about bridges. Use strategies on pages 3 and 4 to help.

**CHART 1**

| Ranking | Bridge | Length (in feet) | Year Completed | Traffic | Country/ Region |
|---|---|---|---|---|---|
| 1 | Danyang-Kunshan Grand Bridge | | 2010 | High-speed rail | China |
| 2 | Changhua-Kaohsiung Viaduct | 516,132 | 2007 | | Taiwan |
| 3 | | 373,000 | 2010 | High-speed rail | China |
| 4 | Weinan Weihe Grand Bridge | | 2008 | High-speed rail | China |
| 5 | | 177,000 | 2000 | Road | Thailand |
| 6 | Beijing Grand Bridge | 157,982 | | High-speed rail | China |
| 7 | Lake Pontchartrain Causeway | 126,122 | 1956 (southbound) 1969 (northbound) | Highway | United States |
| 8 | Manchac Swamp Bridge | | 1979 | Highway | United States |
| 9 | | 117,493 | 2007 | High-speed rail | China |
| 10 | Hangzhou Bay Bridge | 117, 037 | | Express-way | China |
| 11 | Runyang Bridge | | 2005 | Express-way | China |
| 12 | Donghai Bridge | 106,600 | 2005 | | China |
| 13 | Shanghai Maglev Line | 98,123 | 2003 | Maglev | China |
| 14 | Dwarka Sector 8 Metro Station-Rama Krishna Ashram Marg Metro Station | 97,795 | 2005–2010 | | India |
| 15 | Atchafalaya Basin Bridge | | 1973 | Highway | United States |

Data from https://en.wikipedia.org/wiki/List_of_longest_bridges_in_the_world

**CHART 2**

| Ranking | Bridge | Length (in feet) | Year Completed | Traffic | Country/ Region |
|---|---|---|---|---|---|
| 1 | Danyang-Kunshan Grand Bridge | 540,700 | | High-speed rail | China |
| 2 | Changhua-Kaohsiung Viaduct | 516,132 | 2007 | High-speed rail | |
| 3 | Tianjin Grand Bridge | | 2010 | High-speed rail | China |
| 4 | Weinan Weihe Grand Bridge | 261,588 | 2008 | | China |
| 5 | Bang Na Expressway | | 2000 | Road | Thailand |
| 6 | | 157,982 | 2010 | High-speed rail | China |
| 7 | Lake Pontchartrain Causeway | 126,122 | 1956 (southbound) 1969 (northbound) | Highway | United States |
| 8 | | 120,440 | 1979 | Highway | United States |
| 9 | Yangcun Bridge | 117,493 | | High-speed rail | China |
| 10 | Hangzhou Bay Bridge | 117, 037 | 2007 | | China |
| 11 | Runyang Bridge | 116,990 | | Express-way | China |
| 12 | Donghai Bridge | | 2005 | Express-way | China |
| 13 | Shanghai Maglev Line | 98,123 | 2003 | Maglev | China |
| 14 | Dwarka Sector 8 Metro Station-Rama Krishna Ashram Marg Metro Station | 97,795 | 2005–2010 | Rail | |
| 15 | | 96,100 | 1973 | Highway | United States |

Data from https://en.wikipedia.org/wiki/List_of_longest_bridges_in_the_world.

## Part 3: Architecture as a Science

### Pre-Speaking Activities

Most people notice what a building looks like when it is built. Not everyone thinks about the technical work that goes into constructing a building. Architecture includes aspects of science that not only make the building visually appealing but also functional to the people who will later use the building. Answer these questions with a partner.

1. What are some steps an architect might follow when planning a building?

   _____

   _____

   _____

2. What are some processes in your field of interest that require you to follow steps?

   _____

   _____

3. Do you like the technical aspect of your field?

   _____

   _____

   _____

4. What types of practical things might conflict with designing the most beautiful building in the world? What might conflict with a process you follow in your own field?

   _____

   _____

# Presentation Strategy: Using Process Words and Phrases

Speakers often use signal words to let you know the steps in a process or when things will happen. It is a good idea to notice these words because they can help you organize the content of a speech or discussion in which you are explaining how to do something.

*Process Words and Phrases*

- **first, second, third, another, next**

  To major in architecture, **first,** talk to your advisor.

  The **second** thing you should do is enroll in the Introduction to Architecture course.

  **Third,** talk to a professional architect to learn more about the job.

  **Another** thing to do is look at Architecture 161.

- **before, during, after/afterward, later**

  **Before** changing your major, you should talk to your advisor.

  The instructor will talk about the history of architecture **during** the lecture.

  There will be an examination **after** the course.

  We'll have a review session **later.**

- **in the past, in the future, used to be, currently, now**

  **In the past,** architects were responsible for all aspects of a building.

  No one knows how the study of architecture will change **in the future.**

  It **used to be** that one architect managed the whole project.

  **Currently/Now,** some architects specialize on one aspect.

- **meanwhile**

  One architect is working on the design. **Meanwhile,** his partner is working on the measurements.

- **yesterday, today, tomorrow**

  The material we covered **yesterday** will be covered on the test.

  There is a study session **today.**

  Be prepared for the test **tomorrow.**

What others can you think of to add to the lists?

## Preparing a Short Speech: Process

Think of something you know how to do that you can teach someone else to do. For example, you might think of building a paper airplane, cooking a special recipe, or using a particular study strategy. You may also choose a process related to your field of study. Use the space to take notes, and then draft a two- to three-minute speech teaching the rest of the class how to do it. Use process words and phrases. Give your speech on the day assigned by your instructor.

_____

_____

_____

_____

_____

_____

_____

_____

_____

_____

_____

_____

_____

_____

_____

_____

_____

_____

_____

## In-Depth Discussion

Work with a small group. Imagine your architectural firm has been offered the chance to develop a new hotel. Work together and think about the art and science that is needed for your hotel. Prepare a presentation that addresses these questions.

1. What are the specifications? (how many floors and rooms, length, width?)

   _____

   _____

2. What is the schedule? (how long will it take, when do you expect to complete it)

   _____

   _____

3. What does it look like from the outside?

   _____

   _____

4. What materials are required for construction?

   _____

   _____

5. Where is it located?

   _____

6. How much will it cost? (budget considerations)

   _____

   _____

7. What are some of the challenges you expect during construction?

   _____

   _____

8. Does it serve any functions other than housing (restaurants, gyms, apartments, shopping)?

   _____

   _____

9. What is the name of the hotel?

   _____

# Rapid Vocabulary Review

From the three answers on the right, circle the one that best explains, is an example of, or combines with the vocabulary item on the left as it is used in this unit.

| Vocabulary | Answers | | |
|---|---|---|---|
| Synonyms | | | |
| 1. absolute | lawful | complete | proven |
| 2. guidelines | rules | ideas | suggestions |
| 3. compromise | promise | demand | agreement |
| 4. practical | reasonable | imagined | possible |
| 5. construct (v) | design | flatten | assemble |
| 6. aspects | facets | appearances | ideas |
| 7. floors | weights | levels | measurements |
| 8. particular | specific | interesting | different |
| Combinations and Associations | | | |
| 9. tag _____ | along | with | around |
| 10. focus _____ | to | on | from |
| 11. break the _____ | ice | foundation | project |
| 12. _____ into | look | hear | see |
| 13. an oldie, but a _____ | newbie | gold one | goodie |
| 14. _____ some coffee | grab | take | drink |
| 15. brought _____ | up | off | under |
| 16. talking _____ | at | with | about |

## Vocabulary Log

To increase your vocabulary knowledge, write a definition or translation for each vocabulary item. Then write an original phrase, sentence, or note that will help you remember the vocabulary item. The log includes 15 items from this unit and allows space for you to add 10 more from your discussions in this class or any other classes.

| Vocabulary Item | Definition or Translation | Your Original Phrase, Sentence, or Note |
|---|---|---|
| 1. amazing | surprising, astonishing | The amazing thing is that no one knew the answer. |
| 2. actual | | |
| 3. structure | | |
| 4. curious | | |
| 5. encourage | | |
| 6. convey | | |
| 7. posture | | |
| 8. familiar | | |
| 9. blend | | |
| 10. functional | | |
| 11. specifications | | |
| 12. considerations | | |
| 13. budget | | |

| Vocabulary Item | Definition or Translation | Your Original Phrase, Sentence, or Note |
|---|---|---|
| 14. visually | | |
| 15. applied | | |
| 16. | | |
| 17. | | |
| 18. | | |
| 19. | | |
| 20. | | |
| 21. | | |
| 22. | | |
| 23. | | |
| 24. | | |
| 25. | | |

# 2

# Marketing: Product Management

Marketing is an important part of business. It involves many disciplines, including psychology, sociology, mathematics, and other business areas. Marketing helps companies decide which products or services are important to people and how to make them interesting to their customers. The marketing process is important not only to make sure customers are happy but also to ensure that the company makes money from sales.

# Part 1: Branding

## Pre-Speaking Activities

A brand is a symbol, a name, a color, or a slogan for a company, product, or service. Most companies want their brand to be famous and recognized around the world so that customers who see or hear the brand will associate it with a company's products, services, or even its personality. Answer these questions with a partner.

1. What are your favorite brands?

_____

_____

_____

2. "Just Do It" is a slogan that Nike has used. What other slogans can you think of?

_____

_____

_____

3. List some companies or businesses you recognize from their brands.

_____

_____

_____

## Strategy: Giving Advice

In English, people often ask for advice. They might ask about social situations (which restaurant to go to), academic contexts (which class to take), or professional input (best way to complete a job task). There are several ways speakers can give advice. You need to deliver advice carefully and think about who is talking and what the content is to make sure your listener knows when you are simply giving advice and when you are actually telling someone what to do.

### Giving Advice (in approximate order of strength)

You had better
I recommend
Maybe you should
You might want to
You have to
You have to be careful that
If I were you
I would
You might want to (wanna)
Why don't you
You could
It seems to me
How about if you

### Giving Advice in the Negative (in approximate order of strength)

I don't think you should
I wouldn't
You shouldn't
You don't have to
You don't need/want to
You wouldn't want to

### Pronunciation Note

Intonation is very important. Although advice is sometimes worded as a suggestion or recommendation, it is really a command or order, especially when a professor is "giving advice" to a student. In such cases, each word is stressed and the statement has falling intonation. When you do not want to sound too forceful: do not stress each word evenly; think about your tone; and use one of the less forceful phrases before your actual advice.

**Command:** You should study every night.
**Less Forceful:** If I were you, I would study every night.

## Giving Advice

Read these situations. Decide what advice you would offer. Begin with a phrase from the list on page 26. Consider who the interaction is between as you choose your phrase. Then compare your answers with a partner or small group. Talk about why you chose the advice as well as how you decided on the strength of your phrasing. Practice delivering the advice, choosing your tone carefully to convey meaning.

| Participants | Situation | Advice Phrasing | Advice |
|---|---|---|---|
| Two students | One student is asking for ways to improve his/her English. | | |
| Student/English teacher | The student is asking for ways to improve his/her presentation for class. | | |
| Two interns at a company | One intern at a summer job is asking a peer how to ask for a day off. | | |
| Intern/Boss | The intern is asking the boss at the office what he/she should do to get a full-time job after college. | | |
| Roommates | One roommate is asking the other about ways to ask someone for a date. | | |
| Student/Professor | The student is asking a professor who teaches in his/her major how to improve a research paper. | | |
| Student/Advisor | The student is asking an academic advisor about what to do with a class that seems too hard. | | |
| Student/Teaching Assistant | The student is asking the TA how to study for the professor's midterm. | | |

Now write two situations. Ask the members of your group to offer advice. Write the phrasing and advice they offer. Then talk about why they chose that phrasing and advice.

| Participants | Situation | Advice Phrasing | Advice |
|---|---|---|---|
|  |  |  |  |
|  |  |  |  |

# Speaking

## Asking for Advice

Sometimes you want to get advice from someone else. There are some formal and informal ways to ask, depending on the person and situation.

| Formal | Informal |
|---|---|
| What would you recommend?<br>Where do you recommend I go?<br>Which professor do you recommend? | What should/do I do? |
| What do you suggest? | Any ideas? |
| Do you think this is okay? | What do you think?<br>What do you think is best? |
| What do you think I should do? | I was wondering, should I [do something]? |
| What would you do?<br>If it was/were you, what would you do?<br>How would you do it? | Help. I don't know what to do. |

## Asking for Advice

Think about how you would ask for advice using the phrases in the boxes. Answer the questions. Then share your ideas with the class.

1. How would you ask for advice about each of the situations?

    a. a good restaurant for a formal dinner _____

    _____

    b. which computer to buy _____

    _____

    c. how to do develop better study habits _____

    _____

    d. changing your major _____

    _____

    e. the best way to cook chicken _____

    _____

    f. ways to save money _____

    _____

    g. ways to lose weight _____

    _____

2. Who would you ask for advice from each of the situations from Question 1?

    a. _____        e. _____

    b. _____        f. _____

    c. _____        g. _____

    d. _____

3. What words do you use to ask for advice? Use phrases from page 28 or add other phrases to the list.

_____

_____

4. What things affect the advice and/or the response? Does the place or time of the interaction matter? Does the formality of the question affect the response?

_____

_____

_____

## Making Contact

Ask three English speakers for advice about where to take your friends or family when they visit. Take notes on the advice wording you used, the response you received, and the details of the interaction (person's status, age, and gender, the time of day, and the location). Be prepared to discuss your data with the class.

| Your Advice Wording | The Person's Response | Details of the Interaction |
|---|---|---|
|  |  |  |
|  |  |  |
|  |  |  |

## Part 2: Product Differentiation

### Pre-Speaking Activities

Think about the variety that exists for each type of product. For example, there is more than one type of computer, toothpaste, or clothing design. Product differentiation is what marketing professionals do to make their product different from the competition. This list of differences is what a product needs for consumers to think that product is worth having because it is different from others. Answer these questions with a partner.

1. What brand of computer do you have? What is your favorite toothpaste? What brand of clothing do you prefer?

   _____

   _____

   _____

2. Think about two different computers, toothpastes, and clothing items. What makes the two different from each other?

   _____

   _____

   _____

3. What do you think are some differences that marketing professionals use to make their products stand out?

   _____

   _____

   _____

## Strategy: Making Introductions

Sometimes you will find yourself in situations where you have to introduce yourself. For example, you may introduce yourself to the person who sits next to you in a classroom on the first day of class, when you meet professors during their office hours, or when you meet new people at a meeting or a club. You may even introduce a speaker at a meeting or conference. There are several ways to do this.

**Hi, I'm [name].**

**My name is [name].**

Most often, the person will respond with their name and a phrase such as *Good to meet you* or *Nice to meet you*. It is also likely they'll respond with their name and a greeting such as *How are you doing*.

It should be noted that introductions are not always the first thing that you talk about. In other words, there may be a little small talk followed by **By the way, I'm [name].**

1: I heard this class is really hard.
2: Me, too. But it's required for me, so I've got to take it.
1: It's required for me, too. Do you know anything about this professor?
2: My roommate took his class last semester. Says he's tough but fair.
1: Is it true that there is a TA for this course?
2: Yeah. My roommate went to the sessions and said it really helped. I'm going to go to the sessions. You?
1: I'm planning to. Did your roommate have any other advice?
2: He said to form a study group. Would you be interested in that?
1: Definitely. Anything to make this course easier.
2: **By the way, I'm Carlos.**
1: **Hey. I'm Li. Good to meet you.**
2: Yeah, you too. Let's see who else sits with us. Maybe we can get a study group of four.
1: Sounds good.

Sometimes you may have to introduce someone else. When you do this, you should tell the other person the name and something about how you know this person. Then both people will know your relationship to the other and have a little information they can use to continue the conversation.

> **Hi, Carolina, this is my friend Runjie.** She is my lab partner in my Chem 101 class. **Runjie, this is Carolina.** She lives down the hall from me in the dorms.

## Practicing Introductions and Extending Conversations

Work with a partner. For each situation, write a dialogue that either begins with a short conversation and ends with an introduction or begins with an introduction and continues with a short conversation. Be prepared to present one dialogue to the rest of the class.

1. You are on a plane flying to an honor society conference. Someone is already in the seat next to you. Talk to that person.

   _____

   _____

2. You get to a professor's office hours, but there is someone in the office and someone else waiting outside. You don't know this professor very well since this is the first time you've taken one of his or her classes. Talk to the person who is waiting.

   _____

   _____

3. You go to a friend's birthday party, but you don't know anyone else at the party. You go over to the table where the drinks are located. A member of the opposite sex is standing there. Talk to that person.

   _____

   _____

4. You are meeting your English conversation partner for the first time. You've been paired with someone who is much older than you. Start the conversation.

   _____

   _____

5. You like to play basketball, so you joined the intramural team. No one else from your country plays, so you arrive and don't know anyone. The rest of the players are there practicing. Walk up to the other players and start a conversation.

   _____

   _____

# Speaking

## Making Comparisons and Stating Contrasts

In English, speakers sometimes compare and contrast at the same time. Certain words or phrases are used when you are going to point out a difference to someone: Sometimes you do this after someone has given a similarity or positive idea and you need to state a difference or a negative idea. Certain words or phrases are used to compare or contrast two things, and those phrases can be at the beginning or in the middle of the statement.

| Comparison Words and Phrases | Contrast Words and Phrases |
| --- | --- |
| also | alternatively |
| and | although |
| as [big] as | as opposed to |
| as much as | but |
| as well as | contrasts with |
| both . . . and | conversely |
| by the same token | despite |
| compared to | even though |
| either | however |
| have in common | is different from/than |
| in the same manner | is the opposite of |
| in the same way | on the other hand |
| just as | or |
| like/likewise | rather |
| similar/similarly | whereas |
| the same as/the same thing | while |
| too | yet |

Stressing the comparison word or phrase or pausing before and after a word or phrase will indicate to the listener that the speaker thinks the comparison is important.

## Making Comparisons and Stating Contrasts

Work with a partner. List five things you have in common. Write sentences using signal words or phrases from page 34. Then list five differences and write sentences. Share your comparisons and contrasts with the class.

List of Comparisons

_____

_____

_____

_____

List of Contrasts

_____

_____

_____

_____

Your Sentences

_____

_____

_____

_____

_____

# Video: **Comparing and Contrasting**

Listen to the pair of students work together to decide how to prepare for a class project. Discuss the questions in a small group.

**Focus on Language**

1. What words or phrases giving and asking for advice do the students use?
   <u>Note</u>: Don't worry about writing exact words. Refer to the box on pages 26 and 28.

   _____

   _____

2. What are some comparisons the students make? What words do they use?
   <u>Note</u>: Don't worry about writing exact words.

   _____

   _____

3. What are some contrasts the students make? What words do they use? <u>Note</u>: Don't worry about writing exact words.

   _____

   _____

4. Write any phrases or idioms that you are not familiar with. Discuss what they mean and in what type of interactions they are appropriate.

   _____

   _____

## Focus on Tone

1. Is it clear when comparisons and contrasts are being made?

   _____

   _____

2. How can you tell how each person is feeling about the discussion? Describe the intonation used by each student.

   _____

   _____

3. Is each person's tone appropriate? Why or why not?

   _____

   _____

## Focus on Nonverbal Communication

1. What nonverbal cues are used to show how each student feels about ideas from other person?

   _____

   _____

2. Were any of these inappropriate? Why or why not?

   _____

   _____

3. Which student do you think has the most expressive nonverbal communication? Is this good or bad for the interaction?

   _____

   _____

**Summary**

1. Which student uses the best combination of words, tone, and nonverbal communication? Support your answer.

   _____

   _____

   _____

   _____

2. Who would you most want to work with? Why? Who would you rather not work with? Why?

   _____

   _____

   _____

   _____

3. What do you think of the idea to focus on the ingredients? What convinced you this is or is not a good idea? Would you choose something else?

   _____

   _____

   _____

   _____

## Ranking

What qualities do you think a musician or musical group needs to have to sell a lot of their music? How can marketing professionals describe musicians? How are musicians different from each other?

Work with a group and list four qualities of musicians. Then rank them by what you consider to be the most important difference to the least important difference.

**Qualities of Differentiation**

_____

_____

_____

_____

Compare and contrast what you know about the top-selling music artists worldwide. Based on your qualities, rank them in order, starting with the ones that sold the most. It's okay if you don't know who all of them are. Do a quick online image search because you are likely to recognize them when you see a photo.

The Beatles                          Madonna

The Eagles                           Mariah Carey

Elton John                           Michael Jackson

Elvis Presley                        Pink Floyd

Led Zeppelin                         Rihanna

Our Ranking

1. _____        6. _____

2. _____        7. _____

3. _____        8. _____

4. _____        9. _____

5. _____       10. _____

_____

Based on Google search. Other searches may produce different results.

## Part 3: Marketing Mix

### Pre-Speaking Activities

Advertising is a big business. The purpose of advertising is to convince people to use a product. People see advertising everyday in a variety of forms. Some advertisements are directed at a particular group of people; others are placed where the largest number of people can see them. A lot of thought goes into the kinds of advertising used for certain products. Answer these questions with a partner.

1. What is your favorite advertisement? Why do you like it?

   _____

   _____

   _____

2. Other than television commercials, what kinds of advertising can you think of?

   _____

   _____

   _____

3. What are some factors that marketing professionals consider when planning advertisments?

   _____

   _____

   _____

## Presentation Strategy: Using Persuasion Words and Phrases

Speakers often use signal words and phrases to let you know when they are emphasizing an idea and want to convince their listeners that their idea is the best one or the right one. Using these words and phrases will help you persuade your listeners.

These words are often adjectives or adverbs. Some common words are:

| | |
|---|---|
| absolutely | most |
| best | much |
| certainly | notably |
| considerably | obviously |
| especially | particularly |
| extremely | positively |
| greatly | really |
| highly | substantially |
| incredibly | unusually |
| largely | worst |
| many | |

They may also use phrases such as:

**You must believe…**

**You have to agree that…**

**Surely you can see that…**

**Most experts will tell you…**

**Do you really think…**

**Of course…**

**How can you possibly think that…**

Quality is the most important factor in advertising. **Obviously,** a quality commercial will sell more than a poorly made commercial.

**Most experts will tell you that** humorous advertisements are more memorable than serious advertisements.

**Do you really think that** college students will enroll in that elective course?

What other words and phrases can you think of to add to the list?

## Preparing a Short Speech: Persuasion

Choose an item you own that you want to "sell." This item can be anything you want: an item of clothing, a cosmetic item, something from your country, or even a food item from your kitchen. Pick an item you can bring to class on the day of your presentation. Write a commercial selling this product to your classmates. Make sure to differentiate it from other products like it and use persuasion words and phrases to help convince your peers that this is the best product. Give your speech on the day assigned.

_____

_____

_____

_____

_____

_____

_____

_____

_____

_____

_____

_____

_____

_____

## In-Depth Discussion

Work with a small group. Imagine your marketing team has been offered the chance to advertise a new electronic game. Work together and think about the product and the advertising plan. Prepare a presentation that addresses these questions.

1. What is the name of the game? Describe it.

   _____

   _____

2. Who do you expect to buy the game?

   _____

   _____

3. How is it packaged?

   _____

   _____

4. How much does it cost? Will there be any fees to pay?

   _____

   _____

5. What is the branding (symbol, slogan, etc.)?

   _____

   _____

6. Where will you advertise (magazines, television, etc.)? Why are these the best places?

   _____

   _____

7. What percentage of your budget will you spend on each type of advertising?

   _____

   _____

8. Write a commercial for your game.

   _____

   _____

# Rapid Vocabulary Review

From the three answers on the right, circle the one that best explains, is an example of, or combines with the vocabulary item on the left as it is used in this unit.

| Vocabulary | Answers | | |
|---|---|---|---|
| **Synonyms** | | | |
| 1. scene | part | whole | half |
| 2. hilarious | priceless | comedic | earnest |
| 3. whereas | and | but | or |
| 4. claim (v) | announce | affirm | share |
| 5. recommend | advise | advocate | advance |
| 6. angle | curve | judgment | perspective |
| 7. feature | attribute | sign | excellence |
| 8. ensure | weaken | moderate | assure |
| **Combinations and Associations** | | | |
| 9. get a point ___ | across | on | over |
| 10. main ___ | road | way | strip |
| 11. night ___ | bird | owl | worm |
| 12. ___ of mouth | talk | word | sound |
| 13. set ___ | together | away | apart |
| 14. ___ advice | can | give | home |
| 15. a slogan ___ | for an animal | for a company | for a friend |
| 26. associated ___ | to | with | by |

## Vocabulary Log

To increase your vocabulary knowledge, write a definition or translation for each vocabulary item. Then write an original phrase, sentence, or note that will help you remember the vocabulary item. The log includes 15 items from this unit and allows space for you to add 10 more from your discussions in this class or any other classes.

| Vocabulary Item | Definition or Translation | Your Original Phrase, Sentence, or Note |
|---|---|---|
| 1. gross | to make (money) | That movie grossed 100 million dollars. |
| 2. organic | | |
| 3. a fee | | |
| 4. allergies | | |
| 5. flyers | | |
| 6. a slogan | | |
| 7. advice | | |
| 8. consumers | | |
| 9. competition | | |
| 10. standout | | |
| 11. ingredients | | |
| 12. convince | | |
| 13. substantially | | |

| Vocabulary Item | Definition or Translation | Your Original Phrase, Sentence, or Note |
|---|---|---|
| 14. obviously | | |
| 15. largely | | |
| 16. | | |
| 17. | | |
| 18. | | |
| 19. | | |
| 20. | | |
| 21. | | |
| 22. | | |
| 23. | | |
| 24. | | |
| 25. | | |

# 3 Earth Science: Earth's Composition

*Earth science* is a general term for all the sciences that study the planet. Earth scientists study the land, but they also study the oceans and atmosphere. They use parts of other sciences, such as chemistry or biology, and other disciplines, such as math, to study how Earth works and why it looks the way it does. This unit explores Earth's structure and composition, the tools used to study it, and phenomena affecting it.

# Part 1: Global Positioning

## Pre-Speaking Activities

The planet has been studied for centuries. **Geodesy** is an earth science that measures the size and shape of the planet. Although this branch of science has existed for a long time, it has changed with inventions in technology. This branch of earth science gives an address to every point on Earth and makes global positioning possible. Answer these questions with a partner.

1. Have you ever used a global positioning system (GPS)? Where were you? Why did you choose to use it?

   _____

   _____

   _____

2. Do you have a global positing system (GPS) in your car or on your phone? What are the advantages of having a GPS? Are there disadvantages? If so, what are they?

   _____

   _____

   _____

3. How do you think geodesy will change in the future?

   _____

   _____

   _____

# Strategy: Telling a Story

People tell stories. Professors even include stories in their lectures sometimes. Stories are a big part of academic discussions and casual conversations as well. They add examples and interesting facts. The facts might be surprising, unusual, funny, or new. There are certain words and phrases you can use to make your stories interesting.

**As a matter of fact**

**As funny as it sounds**

**Interestingly (enough)**

**Believe it or not,**

**Funny thing,**

**The thing is . . . .**

**Oddly,**

**Surprisingly/Surprising,**

**This sounds [strange/crazy], but . . . .**

**Strange/Strangely,**

**It all boils down to . . . .**

**The crux of the matter . . . .**

**More than anything else,**

**Remember what I said earlier.**

**You wouldn't believe it, but . . . .**

**You won't believe what happened next.**

**Interestingly enough,** no one really knows when the debate started.

**Oddly,** the test did not show the results they expected.

**As funny as this sounds,** I really want to study on Friday night.

## Pronunciation Note

Phrases that precede interesting facts are usually followed by a pause. Then, the content word(s) that is/are interesting, new, surprising, or unusual is/are stressed so the listener knows what is most important.

Believe it or not, [pause] the **BIGGEST** earthquake in 2010 was not the **DEADLIEST.**

## Telling a Story

Answer these questions. Then share answers by telling the stories to a partner.

1. If you were telling a friend about your weekend, what are two interesting things you would include in your narrative?

   _____

   _____

   _____

   _____

2. If you were telling your advisor about a class you are taking, what would you choose to say?

   _____

   _____

   _____

   _____

3. If you were telling your professor why you decided to major in [your field of interest], what would you include in your story?

   _____

   _____

   _____

   _____

# Speaking

## Using the Phone

Most phone calls begin this way:

**Step 1: Open with a greeting.**

**Step 2: Identify yourself.**

You should give your name or let the person know where they know you from. Depending on who you are calling, you may also have to ask for a person or a department. Once you reach the person you are calling, you should complete step three.

**Step 3: State the purpose of your call.**

There are several ways to state the purpose of your call. Starting your reason with a purpose phrase will alert your listener that you're about to say exactly what you need.

| Identifying Yourself | Stating Your Purpose |
|---|---|
| My name is [Charles Timson]. | I'm calling to ask about [the test]. |
| This is [Darrin Michaels]. | I need to find out [when your office hours are]. |
| This is [Nathan Williams], and I am a student in your English class. | I was wondering if you could explain [how to get to your office]. |
| I'm taking your Earth Science 101 class. | I wanted to ask if [the bookstore had any special prices this week]. |
| This is [Lucy], and I'm in your morning class. | I'm hoping to learn [when tickets will be on sale]. |
| I'm [Tim], and my roommate is in your earth science class. | I'm interested in buying [a DVD]. Could you tell me how much [the DVD costs]? |

## Using the Phone

Think about using the phone, and then answer these questions with a partner.

1. What would you say in each situation?

   a. you dialed the wrong number _____

   _____

   b. you need to be transferred to another department _____

   _____

   c. your friend's roommate answers the phone _____

   _____

   d. your instructor's husband answers the phone _____

   _____

   e. you want to file a complaint with the phone company _____

   _____

   f. you need to make a doctor's appointment _____

   _____

   g. you have to get the homework assignment from the instructor _____

   _____

2. What things affect the phrasing you choose? Does the place or time of the interaction matter? Does it matter who you are calling?

   _____

   _____

3. Under what circumstances is it better to call an instructor rather than send an email message?

   _____

   _____

## Making Contact

Make phone calls to your school or from a local college or university to get answers to the questions listed in the chart. Take notes on the responses you receive and as many of the details of the interaction as you can (person's job, gender, the time of day, and the location). Be prepared to discuss your data with the class.

| Office | Question | The Person's Response | Details of the Interaction |
|---|---|---|---|
| Registrar | How much does a transcript cost? | | |
| Athletics | What grade point average is required for student athletes? | | |
| Financial Aid | What is the deadline for financial aid applications? | | |
| Campus Safety | How much does a campus parking ticket cost? | | |
| Transportation | Where is your office located? | | |
| Admissions | What TOEFL® score is required for admission? | | |
| Your Department | Who is teaching _____ next term? | | |

## Part 2: Earthquakes

### Pre-Speaking Activities

Part 1 mentioned global positioning systems to navigate the Earth. Part 2 addresses a natural phenomenon that has affected Earth's surface: earthquakes. An earthquake causes the Earth's crust to shake or roll. It is the Earth's way of releasing stress, but it can change the way things look. Earthquakes can not only alter manmade constructions, but they can also alter the earth itself. Answer these questions with a partner.

1. Have you ever felt an earthquake? Where were you? What was it like?

_____

_____

_____

2. What areas do you know of that are likely to have earthquakes? Would you want to live there?

_____

_____

_____

3. What is the biggest earthquake that you are familiar with? What sort of damage did it do? Did it change the Earth's surface?

_____

_____

_____

_____

_____

_____

# Strategy: Asking for Clarification

Sometimes when people are giving a lot of information, such as during a lecture, or when they can't judge your understanding face-to-face, such as on the telephone, they will ask a question to make sure you understood or got all the information you needed. They are asking for clarification. Doing so is wise because you need to make sure everyone understands. Otherwise, a conversation or discussion can suffer. Deciding when to ask for clarification may depend on the vocabulary, the amount of information, how much the audience already knows about the topic, or some other factor. The speaker decides when to ask. There are formal and informal ways to do this.

*Formal Questions*

Do you understand?/Understand?

Are you following me?

Is that clear?

Do you see what I mean?/See what I mean?

Does that make sense?

Do you know what I mean?/Know what I mean?

See what I'm saying?

*Informal Questions*

Got it?

Are you with me?

Make sense?

Okay?

You know?

### Pronunciation Note

Questions that are intended to check clarification are usually asked because someone really wants an answer. Therefore, when asking one, remember to pause after the question to give people time to answer.

## Asking for Clarification

Think about situations where asking for clarification is important, and answer these questions with a partner.

1. Circle which people you think should use more formal questions to ask for clarification. Explain why or why not.

    a. a professor _____

    b. a roommate _____

    c. a group of classmates _____

    d. friends _____

    e. parents talking to young children _____

    f. adults talking with their parents _____

    g. customer service representatives taking calls for a company _____

    _____

2. What other clarification questions have you heard? Can you add any others to the list?

    _____

    _____

3. What settings or topics do you think require the formality or need for clarification? List as many as you can.

    _____

    _____

## Speaking

### Responding to Clarification Questions

When people check for your understanding, you should let them know if you understand. If you don't, be honest. This is a good time to let them know that you don't understand everything or that you missed a piece of information. You can let the other people know whether you understand even if they don't ask first. Some common phrases to do this are listed.

| Yes, I understand. | No, I don't understand. |
| --- | --- |
| I understand. | I'm not sure I understand. |
| I know what you mean. | Can you say that again? |
| I get it. | I'm sorry./Sorry. |
| Got it. | I don't get it. |
| Makes sense. | What was that? |
| I'm good./I'm OK. | Huh?/What? |

## Asking for and Responding to Clarification Questions

Work with a small group. Choose a box of facts to write about on a separate sheet of paper. Imagine you are the instructor lecturing students about the 1906 San Francisco earthquake. Write sentences based on the facts you have to give to the other members of your group. Ask for clarification when it is appropriate. Be prepared for them to state their comprehension or incomprehension during your lecture. Take turns being the instructor and the student.

---

### Box A

Happened April 18, 1906

One of the most significant earthquakes

Fault rupture was 296 miles along the San Andreas fault

Confused geologists because they didn't have knowledge of plate tectonics

A professor named Reid analyzed the crust and created his elastic-rebound theory of the earthquake source (still the main model of the earthquake cycle today)

---

### Box B

Started with a foreshock at 5:12 AM with the actual quake starting 20–25 seconds later

Epicenter was near San Francisco, but it was felt in Oregon and Nevada

Shaking lasted 45–60 seconds

The highest Modified Mercalli Intensities (MMIs) were from VII to IX

The MMIs were parallel to the length of the rupture and were as long as 80 kilometers

---

### Box C

A professor named Lawson noticed the intensity and geologic conditions were linked

Areas with sediment had stronger shaking than areas with bedrock

Earthquake is most remembered for the fire it started

The earthquake and fire caused over 700 deaths, but the exact number is not certain

Most deaths were in San Francisco, but 189 were reported in other places

---

Data from *U.S. Geological Survey,* "The Great 1906 San Francisco Earthquake, http://earthquake. usgs.gov/regional/nca/1906/18april/.

# Video: Asking for Clarification During an Office Hour

Listen to the student talk with an instructor about an assignment during an office hour. Discuss the questions in a small group.

## Focus on Language

1. Did you notice any phrases that instructor uses to draw attention to something she finds interesting in the story? <u>Note</u>: Don't worry about writing exact words. Refer to the box on page 49.

   _____

   _____

2. What phrases asking for clarification did you hear? <u>Note</u>: Don't worry about writing exact words. Refer to the box on page 56.

   _____

   _____

3. How does the student state her understanding? <u>Note</u>: Don't worry about writing exact words. Refer to the box on page 58.

   _____

   _____

4. The professor makes a telephone call. Did she follow all three steps listed on page 51? How?

   _____

   _____

5. Write any phrases or idioms that you are not familiar with. Discuss what they mean and in what types of interactions they are appropriate.

   _____

   _____

## Focus on Tone

1. Does the student really understand the assignment? Support your answer.

   _____

   _____

2. Does the instructor always leave enough time after asking for clarification?

   _____

   _____

3. Is each person's tone appropriate? Why or why not?

   _____

   _____

## Focus on Nonverbal Communication

1. What nonverbal cues are used? Who do you think is the most expressive?

   _____

   _____

2. Was any nonverbal communication inappropriate? Why or why not?

   _____

   _____

3. What other types of nonverbal cues could be added?

   _____

   _____

**Summary**

1. Do you think this instructor did a good job of making sure the student understands? Why or why not?

   _____

   _____

   _____

   _____

2. What do you think is interesting about the assignment?

   _____

   _____

   _____

   _____

3. What do you think is most interesting about this interaction? How is this similar to or different from office hour interactions you have had?

   _____

   _____

   _____

   _____

## Information Gap

Earthquakes have been taking place around the world for centuries. Many people are aware of the Richter scale, which measures the magnitude. However, that is not the only way to measure an earthquake. Scientists also measure earthquakes by their intensity. To measure the intensity, they use the Modified Mercalli Intensity Scale.

Work with a partner to complete the chart describing the intensity. Person A has Chart 1 on page 63. Person B has Chart 2 on page 64. Work back to back to complete the information. Ask for more information or clarification if you need to.

**CHART 1**

| Intensity | Shaking | Verbal Description | Magnitude | Observations |
|---|---|---|---|---|
| I | | Instrumental | 1 to 2 | Not felt |
| II | Weak | Feeble | 2 to 3 | Felt by few people at rest and/or on upper floors |
| III | Weak | Slight | | Felt noticeably by people indoors and/or on upper floors |
| IV | Light | | 4 | Felt indoors by many, felt outdoors by few |
| V | Moderate | Rather strong | 4 to 5 | |
| VI | | Strong | 5 to 6 | Felt by all (many frightened) |
| VII | Very strong | Very strong | | Damage negligible in well-built structures; damage considerable in poorly-built structures |
| VIII | Severe | Destructive | 6 to 7 | Damage slight in specially built structures; damage great in poorly built structures |
| IX | Violent | | 7 | Damage considerable in specially designed structures; damage great in substantial buildings with partial collapse |
| X | Extreme | Disastrous | | Destruction of well-built wooden structures or masonry and frame structures |

Information compiled from: http://earthquake.usgs.gov/learn/topics/mercalli.php
http://www.geography-site.co.uk/pages/physical/earth/richt.html

**CHART 2**

| Intensity | Shaking | Verbal Description | Magnitude | Observations |
|-----------|---------|--------------------|-----------|--------------|
| I | Not felt | | 1 to 2 | Not felt |
| II | Weak | Feeble | 2 to 3 | Felt by few people at rest and/or on upper floors |
| III | | Slight | 3 to 4 | Felt noticeably by people indoors and/or on upper floors |
| IV | Light | Moderate | | Felt indoors by many, felt outdoors by few |
| V | Moderate | | 4 to 5 | Felt by nearly everyone |
| VI | Strong | Strong | 5 to 6 | |
| VII | | Very strong | 6 | Damage negligible in well-built structures; damage considerable in poorly-built structures |
| VIII | Severe | Destructive | 6 to 7 | Damage slight in specially built structures; damage great in poorly built structures |
| IX | Violent | Ruinous | | Damage considerable in specially designed structures; damage great in substantial buildings with partial collapse |
| X | Extreme | | 7 to 8 | Destruction of well-built wooden structures or masonry and frame structures |

Information compiled from http://earthquake.usgs.gov/learn/topics/mercalli.php and http://www.geography-site.co.uk/pages/physical/earth/richt.html.

## Part 3: Types of Rocks

## Pre-Speaking Activities

The Earth is made of rock, and there are many types of rocks. Surprisingly, most rocks on the surface are formed from only eight elements. However, those eight elements can be combined in many ways to make rocks look very different. For this reason, many people collect rocks. Answer these questions with a partner.

1. Would you ever be interested in collecting rocks? Do you have any collections? What do you collect?

_____

_____

_____

2. Why did you choose to collect what you did?

_____

_____

_____

3. What is the most interesting item in your collection?

_____

_____

_____

## Presentation Strategy: Adding Examples

The first part of Unit 3 talked about telling a story and adding interesting facts. These can make a presentation more interesting. Another way to make a presentation more interesting is by adding examples. Examples can also make the content easier to understand. For instance, professors sometimes add examples to lectures to make the technical or academic content easier. You can use certain words or phrases to let your listeners know when you are giving examples.

Study these words and examples from someone giving a presentation on his or her rock collection.

*Classification (Example) Signal Words and Phrases*

- **categories, characteristics, classes, classifications, divisions, groups, kinds, parts, types, sections, sorts**

    - Rocks fall into three basic **categories:** igneous, sedimentary, and metamorphic.

    - There are three **classes** of rocks: igneous, sedimentary, and metamorphic. Also, each of those **classes** has many examples within it.

- *for example, for instance*

    - **For example,** oxygen is an element that often found in rocks.

    - Volcanoes produce igneous rocks; **for instance,** pumice.

- *much like*

    - Sedimentary rocks are **much like** the rocks you see every day on campus near the fountain by the bookstore.

- *the following*

    - **The following** are examples of common elements found in rocks: oxygen, iron, and aluminum.

- *such as*

    - Rocks, in general, are primarily comprised from one or more of eight elements, **such as** oxygen, iron, or aluminum.

- *specifically, particularly*

  - Eight elements make up rocks. **Specifically,** one common element in many rocks is oxygen.

  - Eight elements make up rocks. **Particularly,** oxygen is a common element in many kinds of rocks.

- *illustrated by, to illustrate*

  Igneous rocks are made from volcanoes. **To illustrate,** think about basinite, basalt, or pumice.

What others can you think of to add to the lists?

### Pronunciation Note

In English, it is important to clearly pronounce the final -s sound on plural nouns. Although the listener will likely understand what you mean from the context, the sentence will not sound grammatical and you will not sound academic or professional, which can affect your grade or audience response when you are giving a speech or presentation.

For example, the listener knows the word **types** is plural in this sentence:

There are three **types** of rocks.

However, if you don't say the final -s sound clearly enough, the sentence sounds like this:

There are three **type** of rocks.

To say the *-s* sound, the tip of your tongue should be near the back of your top teeth, but it should not touch your teeth. In fact, your tongue should not touch the roof of your mouth either. You blow air between your teeth and your tongue to make a hissing sound.

## Listening for and Using Examples

Work with a group. Look at the categories listed. Think of three examples to fit into each category. Then write sentences using example signal words or phrases. Present your lists to the other groups.

1. private or public companies

_____

_____

_____

2. humanities disciplines

_____

_____

_____

3. types of sciences

_____

_____

_____

4. best places to study on campus

_____

_____

_____

5. benefits of learning a new language

_____

_____

_____

## Preparing a Short Speech: Narrative

Think of a seminar or talk you attended, a guest speaker you heard, an academic discussion you participated in, or a lecture you attended for another class. You may also consider a lecture you watched online or on television. Use this space to take notes and draft a narrative (story) about five or six minutes long that tells the rest of the class about the content. Remember to include storytelling words and phrases and check for comprehension throughout your speech. Give your speech on the day assigned by your instructor.

_____

_____

_____

_____

_____

_____

_____

_____

_____

_____

_____

_____

_____

_____

_____

## In-Depth Discussion

Work with a small group. Imagine you have the chance to take a trip around the world to see what the planet Earth has to offer. Work with your team to create an itinerary of places. Create your list based on these categories. Try to think of at least two examples for each category.

1. places to see volcanoes _____

_____

2. the places most likely to experience an earthquake _____

_____

3. the best places to see a lot of rocks _____

_____

4. the best places to experience the Earth's oceans _____

_____

5. the best places to see the stars (or into outer space) _____

_____

6. the most dangerous places on the planet _____

_____

7. the places with the best mountains _____

_____

8. the oldest places _____

_____

9. the hottest places _____

_____

10. the coldest places _____

_____

# Rapid Vocabulary Review

From the three answers on the right, circle the one that best explains, is an example of, or combines with the vocabulary item on the left as it is used in this unit.

| Vocabulary | Answers | | |
|---|---|---|---|
| Synonyms | | | |
| 1. an assignment | dangerous | homework | sleeping |
| 2. location | person | place | thing |
| 3. one sort | one belief | one noise | one type |
| 4. atmosphere | air | birthday | beverage |
| 5. a phrase | group of letters | group of sounds | group of words |
| 6. facet | part | appearance | time |
| 7. relevant | pertinent | frivolous | admission |
| 8. odd | excellent | many | strange |
| Combinations and Associations | | | |
| 9. find out ___ | food | information | rain |
| 10. ___ an appointment | do | make | run |
| 11. such ___ | as | in | of |
| 12. a complaint about ___ | an excellent flight | a great test | a noisy neighbor |
| 13. a branch of a ___ | person | chair | discipline |
| 14. damage ___ | to your breakfast | to your house | to your pencils |
| 15. depend ___ | of | on | out |
| 16. a wrong ___ | cheese | number | umbrella |

## Vocabulary Log

To increase your vocabulary knowledge, write a definition or translation for each vocabulary item. Then write an original phrase, sentence, or note that will help you remember the vocabulary item. The log includes 15 items from this unit and allows space for you to add 10 more from your discussions in this class or any other classes.

| Vocabulary Item | Definition or Translation | Your Original Phrase, Sentence, or Note |
|---|---|---|
| 1. phenomena | extraordinary things | Falling stars are astronomical phenomena. |
| 2. boil down | | |
| 3. narrative | | |
| 4. alter | | |
| 5. theory | | |
| 6. significant | | |
| 7. combine | | |
| 8. measure (v.) | | |
| 9. the magnitude | | |
| 10. a geologist | | |
| 11. a category | | |
| 12. a cue | | |
| 13. illustrate | | |

| Vocabulary Item | Definition or Translation | Your Original Phrase, Sentence, or Note |
|---|---|---|
| 14. intensity | | |
| 15. element | | |
| 16. | | |
| 17. | | |
| 18. | | |
| 19. | | |
| 20. | | |
| 21. | | |
| 22. | | |
| 23. | | |
| 24. | | |
| 25. | | |

# 4

# U.S. History: Presidents

History is a record of the past for any event, people, or place that involved humans. People who study history are called historians, and they record who, what, where, when, and why events took place. This unit will discuss some important people in U.S. history— namely Presidents Lincoln, Kennedy, and Nixon—and how events during their presidencies helped shape the United States.

# Part 1: Abraham Lincoln

## Pre-Speaking Activities

Abraham Lincoln was the 16th president of the United States. He served from 1861 to 1865, when he was shot by an actor named John Wilkes Booth. Lincoln worked a variety of different jobs, had a family, and started a law career before entering politics. He is considered by many to have been one of the best U.S. presidents. He is one of the four presidents whose image was carved into rock at Mount Rushmore. Answer these questions with a partner.

1. Have you heard of Abraham Lincoln? What do you already know about him?

   _____

   _____

   _____

2. What qualities or experience does a person need to be a good president?

   _____

   _____

   _____

3. What other presidents can you name? Were they considered to be as good as Lincoln? Why or why not?

   _____

   _____

   _____

# Strategy: Recognizing Guesses and Expressing Certainty

Sometimes you may not be sure of the information you are going to share. It's okay to take a guess, but you need to let the listener know that you're not certain. Likewise, when you're listening, you need to recognize when someone is not certain. This affects how you take notes and decide what information is the most important. There are certain phrases that are used before a statement that indicate when someone may be taking a guess or when someone is simply offering an opinion.

*Taking a Guess*

> I'd guess he/she/it is/was
>
> I'd guess that
>
> I'd say he/she/it means
>
> It might be
>
> I think it's [partly] because
>
> It looks/sounds like
>
> Perhaps/Maybe
>
> I'm not sure/don't know, but
>
> It could be [due to]
>
> I'm just guessing that it's/My guess is
>
> I wonder
>
> That might be

At other times you may be certain or fairly certain:

**100% Certain**

> I'm certain/sure that
>
> It is
>
> I know that
>
> I'm positive that
>
> I'm convinced

**Less than 100% Certain**

> I'm pretty sure that
>
> I am not sure it is
>
> Could it be
>
> I'm almost positive that
>
> I think

Pronunciation Note

English words are not always said separately or clearly. Some words are **linked** or joined with the word after it. For example, words that end in a consonant are linked or joined to a word that begins with a vowel. Other links include consonant-to-consonant and vowel-to-vowel. It sounds like one word instead of two or more. Therefore, the phrase *I'd guess it's* might sound like *I'dguessit's*.

Why was Lincoln considered a great leader?

**I'd guess it's because he had military experience.**

**I'd say it's because he was a good speaker.**

**I think it's because he brought an end to slavery.**

## Recognizing Guesses and Expressing Certainty

Read Lincoln's most famous speech, *The Gettysburg Address*. Work with a partner. Divide the reading into two parts. Then follow the steps.

1. Mark the places where linking between final consonant and beginning vowel sounds could occur. Draw lines or highlight them in the text. Then practice reading the speech and linking the words. Exchange parts, and practice linking the words in the other half of the speech.

2. Choose three sentences from your half of the speech, and write what you think Lincoln meant. Begin your statement with an appropriate phrase depending on if you are taking a guess or expressing certainty.

   You can use phrases from the box on page 76 or you can adapt one. Read your statements to your partner.

   a. _____

   _____

   _____

   b. _____

   _____

   _____

   c. _____

   _____

   _____

3. Work on the last long sentence together. What do you think Lincoln was saying? Read your guess to the class.

   _____

   _____

   _____

   _____

   _____

# Transcript of Gettysburg Address (1863)

Fourscore and seven years ago our fathers brought forth on this continent a new nation, conceived in liberty and dedicated to the proposition that all men are created equal.

Now we are engaged in a great civil war, testing whether that nation or any nation so conceived and so dedicated can long endure. We are met on a great battlefield of that war. We have come to dedicate a portion of that field as a final resting place for those who here gave their lives that that nation might live. It is altogether fitting and proper that we should do this.

But in a larger sense, we cannot dedicate, we cannot consecrate, we cannot hallow this ground. The brave men, living and dead who struggled here have consecrated it far above our poor power to add or detract. The world will little note nor long remember what we say here, but it can never forget what they did here. It is for us the living rather to be dedicated here to the unfinished work which they who fought here have thus far so nobly advanced. It is rather for us to be here dedicated to the great task remaining before us—that from these honored dead we take increased devotion to that cause for which they gave the last full measure of devotion—that we here highly resolve that these dead shall not have died in vain, that this nation under God shall have a new birth of freedom, and that government of the people, by the people, for the people shall not perish from the earth.

## Taking Guesses and Expressing Certainty

Think about taking guesses and expressing certainty. Then share your ideas with the class.

1. List three situations when it's okay to take a guess. List three times when you should express certainty.

   _____

   _____

   _____

2. What words do you use to take guesses? To express certainty? Add other phrases to the list and to those on pages 76–77.

   _____

   _____

   _____

3. Are there certain jobs in which people express certainty more than others? Give examples. Is this good, bad, or sometimes good and sometimes bad?

   _____

   _____

   _____

4. What types of things affect a person's decision to take a guess or express certainty? Does the place or time of the interaction matter? Does the formality of the question affect the response? Which phrases are more formal? Which are more informal?

   _____

   _____

   _____

# Speaking

## Giving Your Opinion

There are a few other common ways that people can express their opinions. Make sure to preface your opinion with one of these phrases so others in the discussion or conversation will not think you are stating a fact or expressing certainty.

| Giving Opinions |
| --- |
| As far as I'm concerned… |
| From my perspective… |
| I believe… |
| I think… |
| I would/I'd say/argue that… |
| In my opinion… |
| To me… |
| To my mind… |

Can you think of others to add to the list?

## Giving Your Opinions

Work with a partner. State your opinion about the topics. Take turns going first.

1. Interracial marriage

   _____

2. Where elder family members should live (on their own, with family, retirement homes)

   _____

3. The number of work visas for foreign employees in the United States

   _____

4. Doctor salaries

   _____

5. Taxes on high-calorie, high-sugar drinks

   _____

6. Social networking

   _____

7. Online courses

   _____

8. Working mothers

   _____

9. Equal rights for women

   _____

10. Requirements to be President of the United States

   _____

# Making Contact

Ask each of the questions to a different English speaker. Take notes on the answers, the phrases (if any) used before the answer in the person's response, and the details of the interaction (person's status, age, and gender, the time of day, and the location). Be prepared to discuss your data with the class.

| Question | The Person's Response | Details of the Interaction |
|---|---|---|
| Who do you think was the best U.S. president? | | |
| Who gave the Gettysburg Address? | | |
| Who was president during the Civil War? | | |
| How many men were president of the United States before Abraham Lincoln? | | |
| Why do many people think that President Lincoln was a great President? | | |

## Part 2: Richard Nixon

## Pre-Speaking Activities

Richard Nixon was the 37th president of the United States. During his term (1969–1974), he improved the country's relationships with China and Russia. However, he is remembered mostly because of the Watergate scandal. In 1972, the Democratic Party's office in the Watergate building was broken into, and Nixon, a Republican, was accused of playing a role. The *Washington Post*, a well-known American newspaper, published stories about the Watergate scandal and revealed to the American people that Nixon was involved in this and other similar "tricks" against Democrats. Eventually, Nixon resigned. He was the only president to resign from the presidency. Answer these questions with a partner.

1. What other political scandals have you heard about?

   _____

   _____


2. How do you learn about current events in the news? What newspapers do you read? What TV channels to you watch? What websites do you check? Are they reliable?

   _____

   _____

   _____


3. How much freedom should the press (media) have to report anything reporters think is news? Compare freedom of the press in the United States to other countries that you are familiar with.

   _____

   _____

   _____

# Strategy: Presenting Arguments

In academic discussions, you sometimes have to disagree with someone's opinion. When you do, it's best if you can explain your disagreement and present an argument about why you feel differently. Being able to explain your idea makes it stronger.

There are certain phrases speakers can use to indicate that they are trying to present the other side of an argument or provide details about their ideas.

*Presenting Arguments*

But what about

Don't you agree that

Everyone needs to consider that

I have another [idea/question] we should talk about

The issue is

My point is

The question we need to think about is

Remember that

Well, I think that

What I want to say is

What is important to include is

You're forgetting that

> **My point is** that all citizens have the right to know what the president is doing.
>
> **The issue is** not about informing us what the person is doing right, it's about knowing that the person has done something wrong.
>
> **Don't you agree that** sometimes we know too much about other people?
>
> **You're forgetting that** presidents are elected in the United States, so the people who elect them should know about their activities.
>
> **I have another idea we should think about** in our discussion of the Constitution.

## Pronunciation Note

**Emphatic stress** changes the stress from the main noun to another word. This allows you to emphasize the information you really want your listener to hear.

My point is that **ALL** citizens have the right to know what the president is doing. [not just some citizens]

My point is that all citizens have the right to know what the **PRESIDENT** is doing. [not all people, just the president]

The issue is not about informing us what the person is **doing RIGHT**, it's about us knowing what the person **has done WRONG**.

The issue is not about **INFORMING** us what the person is doing right, it's about us **KNOWING** what the person has done wrong.

## Presenting Arguments

Work with a partner. Discuss each statement. Take turns giving your opinion and presenting an argument about each. For the last five, write your own topics. Use emphatic stress as necessary.

1. Barack Obama was the greatest U.S. president.

2. The Sydney Opera House is the most interesting piece of architecture.

3. McDonald's is the company with the best marketing.

4. The television was the best invention.

5. Adventure movies are better than comedies.

6. _____.

7. _____.

8. _____.

9. _____.

10. _____.

# Speaking

## Interrupting

During a lecture, you listen more and participate less (if at all). Some professors, especially in U.S. colleges and universities, might even allow questions during a lecture. During a discussion, everyone has the right to and should participate. You may have to interrupt to make sure you understood something or to offer your own ideas. Interrupting is okay if it is done politely and at the right time. To be polite, use a friendly intonation and appropriate words. To choose the best time, try to wait until the speaker has finished an idea. You don't want to interrupt in the middle of a sentence if you can avoid it.

There are some polite phrases you can use to interrupt before asking for information or giving your own ideas when possible. Sometimes it is more common to interrupt with one word, especially so you don't miss the opportunity.

| Politely Interrupting | One-Word Interrupting |
|---|---|
| Can I say something? | Ok. |
| Excuse me. | No. |
| If I could stop you, | See . . . . |
| I hate to cut in, but | So . . . . |
| I have something to add. | Well . . . . |
| I'm sorry, but | Yeah. |
| I need to interrupt. | But . . . . |
| Let me jump in. | Wait. |
| Hold on. | |

## Interrupting

Work with a small group. One person in the group chooses a topic and starts to talk. For example, you can talk about what you did over the weekend, a homework assignment, something you saw on television, a current event, or someone you know. You can choose anything you want. The other members of the group will interrupt. They may add a new idea, ask a question, or try to change the topic. The first person should manage the interruption and try to get the topic back to the original topic or back on track. Take turns.

Example:

Student 1: Last night I was trying to study.

Student 2: Excuse me, but what were you studying?

Student 1: For my history midterm. Anyway, so I open my book and my neighbor started making a ton of noise.

Student 3: So . . . . What was it? The TV?

Student 1: No, I think it was the radio. In any case, I didn't get much studying done.

# Video: Discussing an Issue

Listen to the students talk about their history class. Discuss the questions as a small group.

**Focus on Language**

1. Do any students take a guess or seem less certain? What wording do they use? <u>Note</u>: Don't worry about writing exact words. Refer to the box on page 76.

   _____

   _____

2. Do any students express certainty or strong opinions? What words do they use? <u>Note</u>: Don't worry about writing exact words. Refer to the boxes on pages 76 and 81.

   _____

   _____

3. What are some arguments the students make? What words do they use to disagree and present their ideas? <u>Note</u>: Don't worry about writing exact words. Refer to the box on page 85.

   _____

   _____

4. Do any students interrupt? What words do they use? <u>Note</u>: Don't worry about writing exact words. If so, how do they get back on topic?

   _____

   _____

5. Write any phrases or idioms that you are not familiar with. Discuss what they mean and in what type of interactions they are appropriate.

   _____

   _____

**Focus on Tone**

1. Do any students use emphatic stress? Write some examples. Are there examples where you think more emphatic stress would be helpful?

   _____

   _____

2. Could you tell by tone which students were guessing and which sounded more certain? Give examples.

   _____

   _____

3. Which emotions are conveyed?

   _____

   _____

**Focus on Nonverbal Communication**

1. What nonverbal cues are used to show how each member of the group feels about ideas from other group members? About their own ideas?

   _____

   _____

2. Was any nonverbal communication inappropriate? Why or why not?

   _____

   _____

3. Which student do you think has the most expressive nonverbal communication? Is this good or bad for the interaction?

   _____

   _____

## Summary

1. Which student do you think was the most certain? Support your answer.

   _____

   _____

   _____

   _____

2. Which student uses the best combination of words, tone, and nonverbal
   communication? Is that the person you most agree with? Why or why not?

   _____

   _____

   _____

   _____

3. Which student was the most polite? Support your answer.

   _____

   _____

   _____

   _____

## Ranking

Gallup.com is a website that provides data based on surveys, polls, and public opinion research. One ranking the website offers is presidential approval ratings. The presidential approval rating is based on how well people think the President of the U.S. did his job.

Work with a group. Make a list of the U.S. presidents that you think had the highest job approval statistics.

**Our Guesses**

_____

_____

_____

Look at this list of 12 presidents. Rank each in order according to the approval rating when the President left office. Consult Gallup.com or another source to help with your answers. Who do you think is number 1 today?

| | | |
|---|---|---|
| Harry S Truman | Richard M. Nixon | George H.W. Bush |
| Dwight D. Eisenhower | Gerald Ford | Bill Clinton |
| John F. Kennedy | Jimmy Carter | George W. Bush |
| Lyndon B. Johnson | Ronald Reagan | Barack Obama |

**Our Ranking**

1. _____

2. _____

3. _____

4. _____

5. _____

6. _____

7. _____

8. _____

9. _____

10. _____

## Part 3: John F. Kennedy

### Pre-Speaking Activities

John F. Kennedy was the 35th president of the United States. His presidency ended when he was assassinated on November 22, 1963, in Dallas, Texas. Although he was only president for three years, from 1961 to 1963, he made several significant decisions, and his term was marked by events that are still important in the United States today. Answer these questions with a partner.

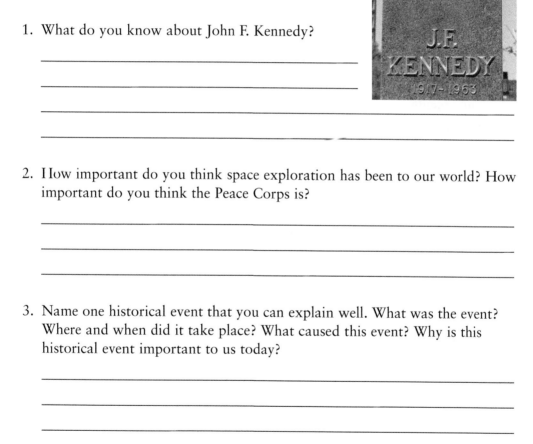

1. What do you know about John F. Kennedy?

   _____

   _____

   _____

   _____

2. How important do you think space exploration has been to our world? How important do you think the Peace Corps is?

   _____

   _____

   _____

3. Name one historical event that you can explain well. What was the event? Where and when did it take place? What caused this event? Why is this historical event important to us today?

   _____

   _____

   _____

# Presentation Strategy: Using Cause-and-Effect Words and Phrases

Speakers often describe important events by explaining who was involved and where and when the event happened. They also describe **how** the event happened and its **cause** (why) and **effect** (the **result** or its significance). They use signal words and phrases to describe those conditions. Using these words and phrases will help make your presentations easier to organize and understand.

*Cause-and-Effect Signal Words and Phrases*

| | |
|---|---|
| as | in order to |
| as a result | resulting from |
| because | since |
| because of | so |
| consequently | so that |
| due to | therefore |
| if . . . then | thus |

> As a boy, Kennedy attended a boarding school in Connecticut, but he got sick. **Therefore,** he had to leave school to recover from his surgery.

> Kennedy's thesis on England was published in part **because** his father wanted him to publish it.

> Kennedy volunteered to be in the U.S. Navy, but, **as a result** of his back problems, he was not accepted at first.

> Kennedy's older brother Joe was going to be the politician in the family. Joe was killed in World War II. **Thus,** John Kennedy ran for Congress in 1948 when James Michael Curley left his seat to become the Mayor of Boston.

What others can you think of to add to the list?

## Using Cause-and-Effect Words and Phrases

Complete these sentences using cause-and-effect signals.

1. If Kennedy had not been assassinated, then . . . .

_____

_____

2. I chose my major because . . . .

_____

_____

3. My advisor recommended three classes . . . .

_____

_____

Write cause-and-effect sentences about each situation.

4. failing a final exam

_____

_____

5. preparing for a job interview

_____

_____

6. freedom of the press

_____

_____

## Preparing a Short Speech: Cause and Effect

Think of a historical or current event that you are interested in. For example, you may be interested in a famous invention, the founding of an organization, or a political conflict. Use this space to take notes and draft a speech of five or six minutes that details the causes and the effects of the event you chose for the rest of the class. Remember to include the language from this unit. Give your speech on the day assigned by your instructor.

_____

_____

_____

_____

_____

_____

_____

_____

_____

_____

_____

_____

_____

_____

_____

_____

## In-Depth Discussion

Work with a small group. Imagine your group is taking historical notes on a former president or leader who is starting his or her own museum. Talk about these details and then present the information about your president or leader to the rest of the class.

1. Who is your leader? Give some details about his or her personal life.

   _____

   _____

2. Where was your leader from, and what country did he or she lead?

   _____

   _____

3. What leadership qualities did he or she have?

   _____

   _____

4. What significant events did your leader manage?

   _____

   _____

5. What important decisions did your leader have to make?

   _____

   _____

6. What were the results of your leader's events or decisions?

   _____

   _____

7. What will your leader be most remembered for?

   _____

   _____

8. Where will the museum be located, and what will it look like?

   _____

   _____

# Rapid Vocabulary Review

From the three answers on the right, circle the one that best explains, is an example of, or combines with the vocabulary item on the left as it is used in this unit.

| Vocabulary | Answers | | |
|---|---|---|---|
| **Synonyms** | | | |
| 1. perish | die | listen | weaken |
| 2. seize | take | leave | start |
| 3. pose (v.) | state | hear | stop |
| 4. scandal | good | equal | bad |
| 5. reveal | not believe | not damage | not hide |
| 6. jeopardize | endanger | make safe | change |
| 7. disseminate | distribute | retain | urge |
| 8. positive | certain | necessary | wrong |
| **Combinations and Associations** | | | |
| 9. ___ a guess | do | let | take |
| 10. disagree ___ someone | at | for | with |
| 11. let me ___ in | choose | jump | precede |
| 12. ___ sure | beautiful | cute | pretty |
| 13. ___ in | split | divide | cut |
| 14. events ___ place | take | make | stay |
| 15. created ___ | equal | same | more |
| 16. run ___ a political office | for | in | to |

# Vocabulary Log

To increase your vocabulary knowledge, write a definition or translation of each vocabulary item. Then write an original phrase, sentence, or note that will help you remember the vocabulary item. The log includes 15 items from this unit and allows space for you to add 10 more from your discussions in this class or any other classes.

| Vocabulary Item | Definition or Translation | Your Original Phrase, Sentence, or Note |
|---|---|---|
| 1. emphatic | strong | The professor's tone was emphatic. |
| 2. endure | | |
| 3. struggle | | |
| 4. portion | | |
| 5. reporter | | |
| 6. resign | | |
| 7. nobly | | |
| 8. consecrate | | |
| 9. in vain | | |
| 10. assassinate | | |
| 11. detract | | |
| 12. devotion | | |
| 13. full measure | | |

| Vocabulary Item | Definition or Translation | Your Original Phrase, Sentence, or Note |
|---|---|---|
| 14. brave | | |
| 15. task | | |
| 16. | | |
| 17. | | |
| 18. | | |
| 19. | | |
| 20. | | |
| 21. | | |
| 22. | | |
| 23. | | |
| 24. | | |
| 25. | | |

# 5 Chemistry: The Elements

Chemistry is a science that studies what objects are made of and how they change when chemicals are involved. The study of chemistry has existed for a long time. Some records date it back to the ancient Egyptians of 4,000 years ago. This unit will talk about chemical elements and how they are studied today.

## Part 1: Green Chemistry

### Pre-Speaking Activities

An element is a chemical substance that has one kind of atom. Some common elements include gold, oxygen, iron, or sodium. To date, more than 115 elements have been discovered. The field of chemistry is always changing. A more recent field is green chemistry. Green chemists want to make the environment better by developing solutions for existing problems. Answer these questions with a partner.

1. What are some ways that people are trying to be greener, such as using solar panels?

   _____

   _____

   _____

2. How do you think chemicals positively and/or negatively affect the environment?

   _____

   _____

   _____

3. What are some chemicals you can name?

   _____

   _____

   _____

# Strategy: Asking for Opinions and Input

In Unit 3, you learned some ways that speakers tell stories and draw
attention to interesting information. You also learned how to ask for
clarification. In Unit 4, you learned that speakers can let you know
when they are taking guesses or expressing certainty and how to express
your opinion. Sometimes in conversations or academic discussions, you
will need to solicit the opinions of others. Hearing from others and
being open to others' ideas often leads to more fruitful discussions.
Questions you can use to ask for opinions include:

*Asking for Opinions*

> **Do you have any feelings about . . . ?**
>
> **How do you feel . . . ?**
>
> **What are your thoughts on . . . ?**
>
> **What do you think . . . ?**
>
> **What's your opinion . . . ?**
>
> I think the earth's biggest environmental problem is pollution. **What
> do you think?**
>
> To my mind, more needs to be done to find other types of fuel. **What
> are your thoughts about this?**
>
> If you ask me, not enough recycling bins are on campus. **What is your
> opinion?**

Can you think of others to add to the list?

## Pronunciation Note

In English words with more than one syllable, one receives more stress than
the others. This is called the **primary** stress. Stressing these syllables will
help you achieve the rhythm of English.

> I feel the earth's <u>big</u>gest en<u>vi</u>ronmental <u>pro</u>blem is pol<u>lu</u>tion.

## Giving and Asking for Opinions

Work with a partner. Take turns asking for and giving opinions on the topics. Review the box on page 81 in Unit 4. Practice using primary stress in words that have more than one syllable.

1. your favorite cafeteria/eating locale on campus

2. the best movie you've seen

3. the hardest general course requirement

4. the easiest way to get to the nearest city

5. the best thing about your hometown

6. texting during class

7. the number of classes you are taking

8. smoking in public areas

9. print versus electronic books

10. global warming

# Speaking

## Asking for an Explanation

When you need more information, you have to ask for it. Do not be afraid to ask for an explanation from someone. This strategy is good practice during any conversation when you need more information, but it is especially important during academic discussions so you can make sure you get more information or understand important information. There are ways to ask indirectly (by using a statement) and directly (by asking a question).

| Statements | Questions |
|---|---|
| I'm not sure I know/understand. | What do you mean? |
| I need more information. | Do you mean . . . ? |
| I don't see why | Can you explain? |
| I can't see a reason for | Why [is that a good idea] [does that happen]? |
| There must be a reason for | Why is that true? |
| I wonder about | What does that mean? |
| I'm curious about | For what reason? |
| I don't get it. | This happened because? (rising intonation on *because*) |
| Hmm | Could you be more specific about that? |
| Excuse me, I'm not following this. | Can you talk a little about that? |
| I don't understand why this is important. | Could you talk more about that? |
| I have a question. | Could you give an example of that? |
| I'd like to know more. | I'm sorry, could I ask one last thing about that one? |
| I'm not sure what that meant. | How?/How come? |

## Asking for an Explanation

Choose an article from a newspaper or a section of a textbook that you have with you in class. Answer the questions.

    Write four specific questions asking for explanations about information in the reading.

a. _____

_____

b. _____

_____

c. _____

_____

d. _____

_____

Work with a partner. Show your selection and share your questions. Then discuss these questions.

1. What kind of information did you decide you wanted an explanation about? Why?

_____

_____

2. Are some phrases on page 105 more formal than others? Which do you consider more formal? Which are less formal?

_____

_____

3. What statements or questions do you use to ask for explanations? Can you add any others?

_____

_____

4. What things affect the phrasing you choose? Does the place or time of the interaction matter? Does it matter who you are asking?

_____

_____

# Making Contact

Survey three people. Ask their opinions about cars. Take notes on their answers and the phrases (if any) they use. Complete the chart, and be prepared to combine your results with four classmates and present those to the class.

| Person's Name | Person 1 _____ | Person 2 _____ | Person 3 _____ |
|---|---|---|---|
| What do you think is the best car to buy? | | | |
| What is your opinion about cars that don't use gasoline? | | | |
| What do you think about the price of cars? | | | |

## Part 2: The Periodic Table of Elements

### Pre-Speaking Activities

Part 1 talked about green chemistry. Part 2 is about the periodic table. The periodic table is a reference that lists all current chemical elements by their atomic number (the number of protons in an atom). Chemists use the periodic table to learn information about individual elements and how they behave. The periodic table is updated when new elements are discovered. Answer these questions with a partner.

1. Have you studied the periodic table before? List any chemical elements you know.

   _____

   _____

   _____


2. The symbol for hydrogen is H. Do you know any symbols for the other elements? List any you know.

   _____

   _____

   _____


3. Do you know of any other fields with a similar list or chart (see page 109)?

   _____

   _____

atomic number → 14 **Si** 28.086 Silicon ← symbol ← name

| | | | | | | | | | | | | | | | | | |
|---|---|---|---|---|---|---|---|---|---|---|---|---|---|---|---|---|---|
| 1 **H** Hydrogen | | | | | | | | | | | | | | | | | 2 **He** Helium |
| 3 **Li** Lithium | 4 **Be** Beryllium | | | | | | | | | | | 5 **B** Boron | 6 **C** Carbon | 7 **N** Nitrogen | 8 **O** Oxygen | 9 **F** Fluorine | 10 **Ne** Neon |
| 11 **Na** Sodium | 12 **Mg** Magnesium | | | | | | | | | | | 13 **Al** Aluminium | 14 **Si** Silicon | 15 **P** Phosphorus | 16 **S** Sulfur | 17 **Cl** Chlorine | 18 **Ar** Argon |
| 19 **K** Potassium | 20 **Ca** Calcium | 21 **Sc** Scandium | 22 **Ti** Titanium | 23 **V** Vanadium | 24 **Cr** Chromium | 25 **Mn** Manganese | 26 **Fe** Iron | 27 **Co** Cobalt | 28 **Ni** Nickel | 29 **Cu** Copper | 30 **Zn** Zinc | 31 **Ga** Gallium | 32 **Ge** Germanium | 33 **As** Arsenic | 34 **Se** Selenium | 35 **Br** Bromine | 36 **Kr** Krypton |
| 37 **Rb** Rubidium | 38 **Si** Strontium | 39 **Y** Yttrium | 40 **Zr** Zirconium | 41 **Nb** Niobium | 42 **Mo** Molybdenum | 43 **Tc** Technetium | 44 **Ru** Ruthenium | 45 **Rh** Rhodium | 46 **Pd** Palladium | 47 **Ag** Silver | 48 **Cd** Cadmium | 49 **In** Indium | 50 **Sn** Tin | 51 **Sb** Antimony | 52 **Te** Tellurium | 53 **I** Iodine | 54 **Xe** Xenon |
| 55 **Cs** Caesium | 56 **Ba** Barium | 71 **Lu** Lutetium | 72 **Hf** Hafnium | 73 **Ta** Tantalum | 74 **W** Tungsten | 75 **Re** Rhenium | 76 **Os** Osmium | 77 **Ir** Iridium | 78 **Pt** Platinum | 79 **Au** Gold | 80 **Hg** Mercury | 81 **Tl** Thallium | 82 **Pb** Lead | 83 **Bi** Bismuth | 84 **Po** Polonium | 85 **At** Astatine | 86 **Rn** Radon |
| 87 **Fr** Francium | 88 **Ra** Radium | 103 **Lr** Lawrencium | 104 **Rf** Rutherfordium | 105 **Db** Dubnium | 106 **Sg** Seaborgium | 107 **Bh** Bohrium | 108 **Hs** Hassium | 109 **Mt** Meitherium | 110 **Ds** Darmstadtium | 111 **Rg** Roentgenium | 112 **Cn** Copernicium | 113 **Uut** Niobium | 114 **Uuq** Ununquadium | 115 **Uup** Niobium | 116 **Uuh** Niobium | 117 **Uus** Niobium | 118 **Uuo** Niobium |
| Lanthanoids | | 57 **La** Lanthanide | 58 **Ce** Cerium | 59 **Pr** Praseodymium | 60 **Nd** Neodymium | 61 **Pm** Promethium | 62 **Sm** Samarium | 63 **Eu** Europium | 64 **Gd** Gadolinium | 65 **Tb** Terbium | 66 **Dy** Dysprosium | 67 **Ho** Holmium | 68 **Er** Erbium | 69 **Tm** Thulium | 70 **Yb** Yttersium | | |
| Actinoids | | 89 **Ac** Actinide | 90 **Th** Thorium | 91 **Pa** Protactinium | 92 **U** Uranium | 93 **Np** Neptunium | 94 **Pu** Plutonium | 95 **Am** Americium | 96 **Cm** Curium | 97 **Bk** Berkelium | 98 **Cf** Californium | 99 **Es** Einsteinium | 100 **Fm** Fermium | 101 **Md** Mendelevium | 102 **No** Nobelium | | |

# Strategy: Using Language to Paint a Picture

Some academic discussions and conversations describe a place or an illustration. To provide a mental picture or help you find something in a physical picture, you should use spatial words or phrases to guide the listeners. There are many words and phrases that describe where something is.

*Spatial Signal Words and Phrases*

| | |
|---|---|
| above | close (to) |
| across (from) | far (from) |
| adjacent (to) | in |
| after | inside |
| at | near |
| behind | next to |
| below | on |
| beside | outside |
| between | to the left (of) |
| by | to the right (of) |
| centered | under |

More than one spatial word or phrase can be used in a sentence.

Neon is **in** the row **below** helium.

Cobalt is **near** nickel and **centered** in the fourth row.

Many spatial words and phrases are used as part of prepositional phrases.

Hydrogen is **at the top** of the periodic table.

Neon is **in the row** below helium.

### Pronunciation Note

In prepositional phrases, the object of the preposition receives the main stress. As a speaker, you need to decide how important the spatial word is. If you use it as part of a prepositional phrase (as in *in the row*), you will not stress it. Therefore, you need to listen carefully for spatial signals.

Nickel is in the fourth **ROW**.

## Using Language to Paint a Picture for Listeners

Write descriptions of the locations using spatial words and phrases. Be as detailed as you can. Then compare your answers with a partner.

1. your dorm room or apartment

_____

_____

_____

_____

_____

2. locations of these buildings on campus: the library, the student union, the bookstore, the registrar's office, your teacher's office

_____

_____

_____

_____

_____

3. directions from school to the closest movie theater

_____

_____

_____

_____

_____

# Speaking

## Stating Correct or Incorrect

When people are explaining or describing something, listeners may want to ask if they have understood something the speaker has said or to question the speaker about something. Some common questions listeners may ask are, "You said X. Is that correct?" or "Did I understand you correctly when you said X?" Speakers will then answer the listener to make it clear if the listener is correct or not. When they do this, tone of voice is extremely important because even if the other person is wrong, speakers don't want to make the other person feel bad. There are many phrases to use when letting someone know if what was understood is correct or incorrect.

| Correct | Incorrect |
|---|---|
| Yes. / Yep. / Yeah. | No. |
| That's right. | No, sorry, that's not right. |
| Right. | Nope. That's not it. |
| Exactly. | Close, but not exactly. Sort of, but not exactly. Kind of, but not exactly. |
| Yes, correct. | Sorry, but . . . . |
| Perfect. | Not exactly, no. |
| Okay. | Nope. |
| You've got it. | Unfortunately, that's not right. |

## Role-Playing

Work with a partner to role-play possible conversations for these situations. Use the phrases in the boxes on pages 105, 110, and 112 or others that you can think of to write dialogues. Then exchange roles. Read your dialogues to the class.

**SITUATIONS**

- providing directions from the classroom to another location on campus

- giving advice on what to do when you have a cold

- describing a process in your field of study

Person A begins by giving directions or advice, describing the process, or listing ideas.

Person B repeats or paraphrases Person A's comments. Person B can also ask for an explanation or more information.

Person A confirms whether Person B is correct or incorrect.

Person A:

_____

_____

_____

_____

Person B:

_____

_____

_____

_____

Person A:

_____

_____

_____

If Person B is incorrect or not exact, Person A can explain again, so Person B has another chance.

# Video: Describing and Confirming

Listen to the pair of students studying for a chemistry test. They are referring to the periodic table of elements. Discuss the questions with a small group.

**Focus on Language**

1. What words or phrases do the students use when they ask for or give an opinion? Note: Refer to the boxes on pages 81 and 103. Don't worry about writing exact words.

   _____

   _____

2. Do any students ask for an explanation? What words do they use? Refer to the box on page 105. Note: Don't worry about writing exact words.

   _____

   _____

3. Where are the elements they talk about on the periodic table?

   _____

   _____

4. What statements for correct or incorrect are used? Refer to the box on page 112. Note: Don't worry about writing exact words.

   _____

   _____

5. List any spatial signal words and phrases you hear. Refer to the box on page 110.

   _____

   _____

6. Write any phrases or idioms that you are not familiar with. Discuss what they mean and in what type of interactions they are appropriate.

_____

_____

## Focus on Tone

1. Who do you think uses the best tone of voice? Why do you like this person's tone best?

_____

_____

2. Is each person's tone appropriate? Why or why not?

_____

_____

3. List the prepositional phrases you hear. Which words are stressed most in the phrases?

_____

_____

## Focus on Nonverbal Communication

1. What nonverbal cues are used to show how each person feels during the discussion?

_____

_____

2. Was any nonverbal communication inappropriate? Why or why not?

_____

_____

3. Which student do you think has the most expressive facial expressions? Is this good or bad for the interaction?

_____

_____

## Summary

1. Which student does a better job of using spatial words and phrases? Give a reason for your opinion.

_____

_____

_____

_____

2. Which student uses the best combination of words, tone, and nonverbal communication? Support your answer.

_____

_____

_____

_____

3. Who would you most want to work with? Why? Who would you rather not work with? Why?

_____

_____

_____

_____

## Information Gap

The chemical elements are organized into the periodic table. The elements are arranged from left to right and top to bottom. They are in order from the lowest to the highest atomic number.

Work with a partner to complete the missing information about the elements in the chart in the first three columns. Complete the last column of the chart together by finding the element in the periodic table on page 109 and describing its location using spatial signals. State if your partner is correct or incorrect as needed. When you're finished, a sample row will look like this:

| Atomic Number | Symbol | Name | Location |
|---|---|---|---|
| 21 | Sc | Scandium | fourth row, third from the left |

CHART 1

| Atomic Number | Symbol | Name | Location |
|---|---|---|---|
| 2 | H | Helium | |
| 4 | Be | | |
| | Mg | Magnesium | |
| 15 | | Phosphorus | |
| | V | Vanadium | |
| 33 | As | | |
| | Mo | | |
| 52 | | Tellurium | |
| 73 | | Tantalum | |
| 84 | Po | | |
| | Rf | Rutherfordium | |
| 112 | Cn | Copernicium | |

**CHART 2**

| Atomic Number | Symbol | Name | Location |
|---|---|---|---|
| 2 | H | Helium | |
| 4 | | Beryllium | |
| 12 | Mg | | |
| | P | Phosphorus | |
| 23 | V | | |
| 33 | | Arsenic | |
| 42 | | Molybdenum | |
| 52 | Te | Tellurium | |
| 73 | Ta | | |
| 84 | Po | Polonium | |
| 104 | | Rutherfordium | |
| | Cn | Copernicium | |

# Part 3: Ocean Acidification

## Pre-Speaking Activities

Depending on who you ask, there are four or five oceans on Earth. These oceans cover approximately 70 percent of the surface. The oceans are important because they affect weather, temperature, and climate change. Although oceans are often studied as part of Earth Science, there are some things about oceans that are studied in chemistry. Answer these questions with a partner.

1. How many oceans do you think there are? List them. Do you know where they are?

   _____

   _____

   _____

2. How many oceans have you seen? If you have seen more than one, did they look or feel the same? Different? If so, in what ways?

   _____

   _____

   _____

3. Do you know what elements are combined to make water? What about carbon dioxide?

   _____

   _____

   _____

# Presentation Strategy: Guiding the Audience Through Your Speech with Change-of-Topic Words and Phrases

Speeches or longer discourse during an academic discussion may be about one topic. However, there may be subtopics. You need to let your audience know when you are moving to a related topic or changing the topic completely. There are signals you can use to change the topic.

*Change-of-Topic Signal Words or Phrases*

**Moving on**

**Now,**

**Speaking of**

**Keep that in mind (as I talk about)**

**That reminds me,**

**By the way,**

**The next [element]**

> Ocean waters cover approximately 70 percent of the Earth's surface. Together they form a connected body of salt water called the World Ocean. Some people say the World Ocean is divided into five smaller oceans. **By the way,** the Pacific Ocean is considered the largest of these. The Pacific Ocean . . . .

> The Pacific Ocean separates Asia and Australia from North and South America. It is the largest ocean. It covers approximately one-third of the surface of the planet and is much larger than all the land on Earth. It's over 63 million square miles. Try to visualize how large that is. **Moving on** to the Atlantic Ocean . . . .

What others can you think of to add to the list?

## Guiding Your Audience

Work with a partner. Look at the chains listed. The first person will state an opinion, give a fact, take a guess, or express certainty about the first item in the chain. The second person will try to make a smooth transition to the next topic in the chain using an appropriate signal word or phrase. Reverse roles. One has been done for you.

| English class | → | Last weekend | → | Job |

A: English class was really interesting today, but we have a lot of homework to do.

B: Speaking of homework, I spent all of last weekend doing homework. It was terrible, especially since I had to work too.

A: That reminds me. I won't be able to study a lot this weekend because I'm starting my new job.

1.  | Oceans | → | Class presentation | → | Roommate |

A: _____

B: _____

A: _____

2.  | Television | → | Football game | → | Chemistry |

A: _____

B: _____

A: _____

3.  | Architecture | → | Academic discussion | → | A social event |

A: _____

B: _____

A: _____

## Preparing a Short Speech: Description

Think of a location you are familiar with. You can choose a personal place, such as your domitory or a room at your house, or a public space, such as a park, the town square in your hometown, or a museum. Use this space to take notes and draft a speech of five or six minutes that describes what this place looks like and why it's important to you. Remember to include the language from this unit as you describe its physical appearance and its meaning to you. Give your speech on the day assigned by your instructor.

_____

_____

_____

_____

_____

_____

_____

_____

_____

_____

_____

_____

_____

_____

# In-Depth Discussion

Work with a small group. Imagine you are part of a team of chemists that has been asked to answer some questions about the future. Think of an answer to each question related to chemistry. When you are finished, take turns serving on a panel to discuss your opinions.

1. What will happen if ocean acidification continues and marine life can no longer live?

   _____

   _____

2. When will there be more vehicles that run on hydrogen or electricity than on gasoline?

   _____

   _____

3. Which chemical element do you think will be the most important in the future? Why?

   _____

   _____

4. What predictions can you make about the future of the environment?

   _____

   _____

5. What three foods do you think are the most acidic?

   _____

   _____

6. What do you think the field of chemistry should study next?

   _____

   _____

7. Do you think all students should be required to take a chemistry class? Why or why not?

   _____

   _____

# Rapid Vocabulary Review

From the three answers on the right, circle the one that best explains, is an example of, or combines with the vocabulary item on the left as it is used in this unit.

| Vocabulary | Answers | | |
|---|---|---|---|
| Synonyms | | | |
| 1. solicit | answer to | ask for | talk to |
| 2. fruitful | good | equal | bad |
| 3. How come? | How? | When? | Why? |
| 4. I don't get it | not understand | not believe | not speak |
| 5. visualize | see | hear | smell |
| 6. public space | your room | a park | your friend's house |
| 7. a vehicle | a number | an element | a car |
| 8. ancient | very nervous | very old | very polite |
| Combinations and Associations | | | |
| 9. periodic ___ | chart | table | list |
| 10. climate ___ | chemistry | change | event |
| 11. ___ to | adjacent | beside | under |
| 12. approximately ___ | the morning | the 1700s | 1,700 |
| 13. that reminds ___ | chemistry | me | the event |
| 14. moving ___ | at | on | by |
| 15. a ___ transition | friend's | nitrogen | smooth |
| 16. X is close ___ Y | from | near | to |

## Vocabulary Log

To increase your vocabulary knowledge, write a definition or translation for each vocabulary item. Then write an original phrase, sentence, or note that will help you remember the vocabulary item. The log includes 15 items from this unit and allows space for you to add 10 more from your discussions in this class or any other class.

| Vocabulary Item | Definition or Translation | Your Original Phrase, Sentence, or Note |
|---|---|---|
| 1. abundant | many, a lot | an abundant supply of money |
| 2. chain | | |
| 3. selection | | |
| 4. green | | |
| 5. behave | | |
| 6. tackle | | |
| 7. oxidize | | |
| 8. curious | | |
| 9. expose | | |
| 10. mines | | |
| 11. peninsula | | |
| 12. lead (n) | | |
| 13. adjacent | | |

| Vocabulary Item | Definition or Translation | Your Original Phrase, Sentence, or Note |
|---|---|---|
| 14. remind | | |
| 15. sodium | | |
| 16. | | |
| 17. | | |
| 18. | | |
| 19. | | |
| 20. | | |
| 21. | | |
| 22. | | |
| 23. | | |
| 24. | | |
| 25. | | |

# Fine Arts:
# Art Appreciation

Art takes many forms, including photography, sculpture, or painting. Different people like different kinds of art. Art appreciation is learning about the art and understanding qualities that make it art. You can look at art from a variety of time periods, artists, and styles and learn to appreciate each piece in its own way, even if you don't like it.

## Part 1: Sculptures

## Pre-Speaking Activities

Sculptures are pieces of art that are 3-D (three-dimensional). Many cultures have a form of sculpture, but they vary in style, color, and/or history. One thing most sculptures have in common is material. Sculptures are often made from a hard material such as stone, metal, or plastic. Because of that, many sculptures last a long time even if they are outside and exposed to bad weather. Answer these questions with a partner.

1. Do you recognize the sculptures? What are they? Where are they located? What are they made from?

   _____

   _____

   _____

2. What other famous statues can you think of? Where are they? Can you find out who the sculptors were?

   _____

   _____

   _____

3. What do you appreciate about each statue that you talked about?

   _____

   _____

   _____

## Strategy: Asking Questions to Fuel Discussion

Whether you are part of a social conversation, an academic discussion, a Q & A session, or an oral presentation, questions play a vital role in the success of an interaction.

People ask questions for two very general reasons:

1. To get specific information
2. To extend a conversation or discussion (show interest)

Sometimes just one question is enough to continue the conversation or discussion. Sometimes several questions might be needed. In either case, questions indicate your interest in extending the discussion or actively participating.

It's not the responsibility of just one person to ask questions. All participants should be prepared to ask questions. If only one person asks questions, then it seems as though others are not interested in the discussion.

Follow these guidelines to ask and answer questions.

- Ask open-ended questions. Use words like *who, what, where, when, why,* and *how* to begin your questions

  **What do you think of Rembrandt's work?**

- Avoid close-ended questions that require short answers.

  **Do you like Rembrandt's work?**

- Give extended answers.

  **Q: What do you think of Rembrandt's work?**

  **A: To me, Rembrandt was one of the best artists of his time; I especially like his interpretation of Biblical stories.**

- Avoid short answers that might be perceived as disinterest or unwillingness to share.

  **Q: Do you like Rembrandt's work?**

  **A: No, not really.**

- Be detailed in questions and answers, especially when you are seeking a specific piece of information.

  **Q: What do you think of Rembrandt's painting *The Night Watch*?**

  **A: I think Rembrandt did something unique by departing from the genre and showed the militia getting ready for battle rather than standing formally in formation.**

- Work to give extended answers, even if the question requires only one word.

  **Q: Who is your favorite artist?**

  **A: My favorite is Rembrandt because he had such great range as an artist. For example, he painted portraits, self-portraits, Biblical scenes, landscapes, and narratives. I like that I can see so many different scenes from one artist.**

## Using Questions to Get Specific Information

Work with a partner. Write questions you would ask in each situation. There could be more than one question to ask for each situation.

1. You are going to go home for the weekend with your roommate.

   _____

2. You need a hotel for your parents when they come to visit.

   _____

3. You want to return the software program you bought at the local electronics store.

   _____

4. You want to know the salary for the internship you applied for.

   _____

5. You want to buy a ticket for the football game.

   _____

6. You need to schedule an appointment with a tutor at the writing center.

   _____

7. You hope to meet with your advisor to talk about courses for next term.

   _____

8. You are hoping to add to your financial aid for next year.

   _____

9. Your friend just had a baby but you don't have any details.

   _____

10. You want to talk to the guest speaker about the university he teaches at because you want to go to graduate school there.

    _____

Work with a partner. Take one situation from the list and write an extended dialogue that begins with the question and leads to a conversation that lasts five minutes. Be prepared to perform your role-play for the class.

_____

_____

_____

_____

_____

_____

_____

_____

_____

_____

_____

_____

_____

_____

_____

_____

# Speaking

## Expressing Positive or Negative Reactions

Sometimes you need to give someone a positive or negative answer. There are many ways to express those. Some are stronger than simply saying yes or no. Others are weaker. Some phrasing is formal, while other phrasing is informal. Remember that you can extend discussions by adding more information after your reaction.

Q: Do you like Rembrandt's work?

A: Not so much. He didn't use many blue or green colors, so a lot of his paintings are too dark for my taste.

| Yes | No |
| --- | --- |
| Absolutely. | No. |
| Definitely. | Nope. |
| It's OK. | No way. |
| Mostly. | Not at all. |
| Sort of. | Not especially. |
| Sure. | Not even a little. |
| Uh-huh. | Not really. |
| Yep. | Not so much. |
| Yes. | Un-uhh. |

**Expressing Positive or Negative Reactions**

Think about times when you have had to give a positive or negative reaction. Then share your ideas with the class.

1. How would you respond if you were asked about each of these things?

   a. a friend's painting:

   you like it _____

   you hate it _____

   b. a Rodin sculpture:

   you like it _____

   you hate it _____

   c. your instructor's lecture:

   you like it _____

   you hate it _____

   d. a new best-selling novel:

   you like it _____

   you hate it _____

   e. your roommate's dinner:

   you like it _____

   you hate it _____

   Rank the terms in the box on page 133 from strongest to weakest. Compare your answers with another group.

   _____

   _____

   _____

   _____

2. What words do you use to give positive reactions? To give negative reactions? Add other phrases to the list and to the box on page 133.

_____

_____

_____

3. What things affect the strength of your response? Does the place or time of the interaction matter? Does it matter who you are talking to or what you are talking about?

_____

_____

_____

## Making Contact

Find a picture of a sculpture. It can be any sculpture you want. Show it to three native English speakers. Ask them if they like it. Take notes on the phrasing you used, the response you received, and the details of the interaction (person's status, age, and gender, the time of day, and the location). Be prepared to discuss your data with the class.

| Person's Response | Positive or Negative? | Details of the Interaction |
|---|---|---|
|  |  |  |
|  |  |  |
|  |  |  |

# Part 2: Painting

## Pre-Speaking Activities

Part 1 talked about sculptures, which are three-dimensional. Part 2 is about another form of art, but one that is 2-D or two-dimensional. Painting is using a brush to add paint, or some sort of color, onto a surface. The word *painting* is both a noun and a verb. It is both the actual act of applying the paint, and it is the result of the act. Answer these questions with a partner.

1. Which painting do you like best? What do you appreciate about it?

   _____

   _____

   _____

2. Can you think of any famous paintings? List as many as you can. Talk about why you think they are famous. Where are they located? Who were the artists?

   _____

   _____

   _____

3. What is the most interesting painting you've seen? Was it in a museum or did someone you know paint it? Why did you like it?

   _____

   _____

   _____

## Strategy: Adding Information

In lectures and academic discussions, and even in casual conversations, speakers may give more than one reason for their opinion or idea. Giving reasons makes your statements stronger, extends discussion, and expresses interest in the topic and/or your desire to actively participate. When used in an oral presentation, reasons help your listeners know when you are giving details or justifying your beliefs. They help you indicate what you want your listeners to hear. Certain words and phrases can be used, especially at the beginning of a sentence.

*Adding Information*

> Also,
>
> And,
>
> Another thing,
>
> Besides that,
>
> Furthermore,
>
> I mean
>
> In addition,
>
> Not only… but also
>
> One more thing,
>
> Plus,

You want to look at Chinese paintings from the Ming Dynasty because artists then used more colors than in earlier Chinese paintings. **Furthermore,** artists from this period began experimenting with new skills.

We're going to write about Leonardo da Vinci. **Not only** was he a painter, **but** he was **also** a sculptor.

### Pronunciation Note

**Reduction** is when sounds are reduced or dropped in spoken English. Sometimes two words sound like one. For example, *wanna* is a reduction of *want to*.

You **wanna** look at Chinese paintings from the Ming Dynasty because artists then used more colors than in earlier Chinese paintings.

We're **gonna** write about Leonardo da Vinci.

## Adding Information

Complete each sentence. Then write a second sentence that begins with adding information signal word or phrase and another reason. Add more than one reason if you can.

1. My favorite painting is _____ because _____.

   _____, _____

   _____.

2. I want to major in _____ because _____.

   _____, _____

   _____.

3. The best artist I've seen is _____ because _____.

   _____, _____

   _____.

4. A great museum is _____ because _____.

   _____, _____

   _____.

5. An amazing sculpture is _____ because _____.

   _____, _____

   _____.

# Speaking

## Making Yourself Clear

Sometimes speakers will say something that isn't clear. Or, they may say something incorrectly. In either case, they can make themselves clear by saying it again in other words or with correct information. There are certain phrases you can use before you make yourself clear. These phrases let your listeners know you are repeating or correcting something you said.

| Repeating |
| --- |
| Basically, I |
| I mean |
| I'm saying that |
| I'm trying to say |
| In other words |
| Let me rephrase that |
| Let me put it another way |
| Maybe I can be clearer if I say |
| To put it another way |
| What I am trying to say is |
| What I mean is |

## Making Yourself Clear

Read the excerpted paragraphs from *The Degas Waxes: An Opportunity for In-Depth Investigation,* an article about Degas from the National Gallery of Art. Choose one sentence from each paragraph, and rewrite both of them to make them clearer for someone. Write your sentences on page 141. Remember that you only have to reword the parts you think are especially hard to understand. Then compare your statements with those of a partner.

(1) *Little Dancer Aged Fourteen,* the only wax sculpture Degas ever exhibited and the most famous of these works, raises numerous questions the Gallery is investigating. "One of our questions is whether the tutu is original. We are comparing it to the inventory photographs, and we will conduct research about the materials from which it is made," says Barbour. "We will also investigate the composition of her slippers, and the wig over which Degas placed wax to form the figure's hair. The wig has always been described as being made of horse hair, but as far as we know no one has ever analyzed it. We can do that now, with the help of our scientific research department, using the Gallery's scanning electron microscope." This microscope, says organic chemist Suzanne Lomax, is capable of high magnification, as well as aiding in material identification. "We can focus on individual particles, and an x-ray spectrometer inside the microscope can tell us what elements are present in that particle."

(2) The scanning electron microscope (SEM) has been particularly helpful in providing information about the composition of the pigments Degas used to tint the wax figures, and the information from these analyses complements the results for pigment identification using polarized light microscopy. [ . . . ] In addition to the SEM, the Gallery's scientific research department uses another instrument, an x-ray fluorescence spectrometer (XRF), to examine the pigmentation of the wax sculptures. This device is capable of providing information on the composition of the surface of an object without the need for taking a sample. "A beam of x-rays pointed at the work of art interacts with the atoms in the piece, enabling you to obtain a characteristic spectrum from which you can identify the elemental composition of the surface material," explains senior conservation scientist Barbara Berrie.

---

Excerpted from National Gallery of Art, *The Degas Waxes,* 2011.

1. _____

_____

_____

_____

_____

2. _____

_____

_____

_____

_____

# Video: Discussing a Topic

Listen to the students work together to prepare for a test in their art class.

## Focus on Language

1. Did any of the students ask questions? Are they seeking information, showing interest, or both? What words did they use? <u>Note</u>: Refer to the box on page 129. You do not need to use exact words.

   _____

   _____

2. What examples of expressing positive and negative reactions did you hear? Which do you think were stronger? Refer to the box on page 133. <u>Note</u>: You do not need to use exact words.

   _____

   _____

3. What words or phrases do the students use before adding information? What words do they use? Refer to the box on page 137. <u>Note</u>: You do not need to use exact words.

   _____

   _____

4. How did the students try to make themselves clearer? Refer to the box on page 139. <u>Note</u>: You do not need to use exact words.

   _____

   _____

5. Write any phrases or idioms that you are not familiar with. Discuss what they mean and in what type of interactions they are appropriate.

   _____

   _____

**Focus on Tone**

1. How can you tell how each person is feeling about the artwork being discussed?

   _____

   _____

2. Which positive reactions were strongest? Negative?

   _____

   _____

3. Is each person's tone appropriate? Why or why not?

   _____

   _____

**Focus on Nonverbal Communication**

1. What nonverbal cues are used to show how each member of the group feels about the artwork being discussed?

   _____

   _____

2. Was any nonverbal communication inappropriate? Why or why not?

   _____

   _____

3. Which student do you think has the most expressive nonverbal communication? Is this good or bad for the interaction?

   _____

   _____

**Summary**

1. Which piece of art do you think you would like best?

   _____

   _____

   _____

   _____

2. Which student uses the best combination of words, tone, and nonverbal communication? Support your answer.

   _____

   _____

   _____

   _____

3. Do you think any of the students could have done a better job of extending the discussion or asking questions? Give an example of both a good and bad moment.

   _____

   _____

   _____

   _____

4. Who would you most want to work with? Why? Who would you rather not work with? Why?

   _____

   _____

   _____

   _____

## Ranking

Have you ever thought about which paintings cost the most money? If you were wealthy and could buy any painting you wanted, what qualities would it have? Make a list of the qualities the painting would need to have in order to make you buy it. Consider subjects, artists, or even colors or textures. Then share your list with a small group.

### Qualities of a Good Painting

_____

_____

_____

_____

Read this list of some of the most expensive paintings ever sold according to Whudat. Do a quick online image search to see what the painting looks like if you are not familiar with it. Then rank them in order from which you think cost the most money to which cost the least. Explain your ranking for the top and bottom choices.

_No. 5_ by Jackson Pollock

_Flag_ by Jasper Johns

_La Rêve (The Dream)_ by Pablo Picasso

_Nude, Green Leaves and Bust_ by Pablo Picasso

_Portrait of Adele Bloch-Bauer I_ by Gustav Klimt

_Silver Car Crash (Double Disaster)_ by Andy Warhol

_The Card Players_ by Paul Cézanne

_The Scream_ by Edvard Munch

_Three Studies of Lucian Freud_ by Francis Bacon

_Woman III_ by Willem de Kooning

1. _____     6. _____

2. _____     7. _____

3. _____     8. _____

4. _____     9. _____

5. _____     10. _____

## Part 3: Photography

### Pre-Speaking Activities

Parts 1 and 2 talked about types of art that most often come to mind when talking about art appreciation. This part is about photography, art capturing objects in still or moving pictures. Although many people use photography to take pictures of special moments, people, or places, some artists capture images that are placed in museums and galleries to be appreciated by many. Answer these questions with a partner.

1. Do you like to take pictures? What do you take pictures of? Do you post them on social media sites? Why or why not?

   _____

   _____

   _____

2. What qualities does a photograph need to warrant its placement in a museum?

   _____

   _____

   _____

3. What is the subject of a favorite photograph you have seen (personal or professional). What did you like about it? What was it?

   _____

   _____

   _____

# Presentation Strategy: Avoiding Stereotypes

A stereotype is a preconceived idea about a person or thing. Stereotypes are often widely held beliefs, usually because some small part of the stereotype is based on fact. Unfortunately, they are oversimplified and not true for all members of the particular group, person, or thing.

For example, the stereotype that men are stronger than women is not altogether false. Many men are physically stronger than women. However, it is a stereotype because there are women who are just as physically strong as men.

Stereotypes are often negative, but they can be positive, too. The stereotype that women are better chefs than men isn't necessarily bad. It's a compliment that many people believe that women cook better. However, it's still a stereotype that isn't true. Think of all the famous chefs that are men: Wolfgang Puck, Gordon Ramsey, Bobby Flay, and Emeril Lagasse.

Whether they are positive or negative, stereotypes should be avoided in discussions so as to avoid hurt feelings or arguments.

There are words and phrases you can use to make general statements and avoid stereotypes. Other words are to be avoided.

| *Use* | *Avoid* |
|---|---|
| A few | All |
| A majority/A minority of | Always |
| Almost | Certainly |
| Approximately | Completely |
| As a rule | Forever |
| Basically | Is/Are |
| Broadly | Never |
| By and large | None |
| Generally | Totally |
| In general | |
| Nearly | |
| Many | |
| Maybe | |
| Most | |
| Seems | |
| Some | |
| Sometimes | |
| Typically | |
| Usually | |

Pronunciation Note

Several vocabulary words you can use end in –*ly*. In some words, when you add a suffix, the syllable you stress changes (**E'**-du-cate vs. **E**-du-**ca'**-tion). That is not true for–*ly* endings. The pronunciation of –*ly* words is easy because the stress remains on the same syllable as the word without the suffix. You simply pronounce the –*ly* word with the stress on the same syllable as the base/original word.

gen'-eral → gen'erally
us'-ually → us'ually

## Avoiding Stereotypes

Look at each commonly held stereotype. Rewrite it to avoid stereotyping.

1. All Americans are fat.

   _____

2. Asian students always get perfect grades.

   _____

3. Men are more aggressive than women.

   _____

4. Engineers are nerds.

   _____

5. New Yorkers are rude.

   _____

6. Great scientists are German.

   _____

7. Children are afraid of spiders.

   _____

8. The English are very law-abiding citizens.

   _____

9. Mexicans learn English easier than the Chinese.

   _____

10. Everyone from South America can dance well.

    _____

## Preparing a Short Speech: Definition

Think of the people who majored in the field you are majoring (or want to major in) or a common concept in that field. For example, if you are an electrical engineering student, you may choose engineers in general as your topic or you may choose a particular concept, such as semiconductors or circuit boards. Use this space to take notes and draft a speech of five or six minutes that defines these people or this concept. Remember to avoid stereotyping and include any other language from this unit or from earlier units to define your topic. Give your speech on the day assigned by your instructor.

_____

_____

_____

_____

_____

_____

_____

_____

_____

_____

_____

_____

_____

_____

_____

_____

## In-Depth Discussion

Work with a small group. Imagine you work for a publishing company and that you want to publish a book of photographs. Answer the questions and then present your publishing plan to the class.

1.  What kind of photographs will you use (color, black and white, matte, glossy, etc.)?

    _____

    _____

2.  What kind of subjects will your book cover (people, places, things, etc.)? Be specific.

    _____

    _____

3.  What characteristics of the photographs do you want people to appreciate?

    _____

    _____

4.  What would be the most unique photograph?

    _____

    _____

5.  What kind of book is it (hard cover, coffee table book, etc.)

    _____

    _____

6.  How much does it cost?

    _____

    _____

7.  Where will it be sold?

    _____

    _____

8.  Who is your target audience?

    _____

    _____

# Rapid Vocabulary Review

From the three answers on the right, circle the one that best explains, is an example of, or combines with the vocabulary item on the left as it is used in this unit.

| Vocabulary | Answers | | |
|---|---|---|---|
| Synonyms | | | |
| 1. literal | exact | likely | somewhat |
| 2. wounded | healed | injured | bandaged |
| 3. as a rule | always | in general | rarely |
| 4. intriguing | interesting | a large number of | ruling |
| 5. vital | minimal | important | equal |
| 6. indicate | point out | generalize | notice |
| 7. complements | helps | praises | pays |
| 8. abide | follow | lead | break |
| Combinations and Associations | | | |
| 9. a ___ of | correction | bunch | grouping |
| 10. be a ___ of | fan | visitor | cheerleader |
| 11. what I meant to ___ | say | speak | tell |
| 12. in other ___ | speeches | words | sentences |
| 13. be ___ to | based | exposed | various |
| 14. not even ___ | a lot | a little | a bit |
| 15. for my ___ | taste | small | sight |
| 16. be capable ___ | of | in | about |

## Vocabulary Log

To increase your vocabulary knowledge, write a definition or translation for each vocabulary item. Then write an original phrase, sentence, or note that will help you remember the vocabulary item. The log includes 15 items from this unit and allows space for you to add 10 more from your discussions in this class or any other class.

| Vocabulary Item | Definition or Translation | Your Original Phrase, Sentence, or Note |
|---|---|---|
| 1. few | not many | a few minutes |
| 2. a sculpture | | |
| 3. a material | | |
| 4. symbolism | | |
| 5. numerous | | |
| 6. by and large | | |
| 7. typically | | |
| 8. heist | | |
| 9. remarkable | | |
| 10. intriguing | | |
| 11. enable | | |
| 12. tidbit | | |
| 13. perceive | | |

| Vocabulary Item | Definition or Translation | Your Original Phrase, Sentence, or Note |
|---|---|---|
| 14. speculate | | |
| 15. genre | | |
| 16. | | |
| 17. | | |
| 18. | | |
| 19. | | |
| 20. | | |
| 21. | | |
| 22. | | |
| 23. | | |
| 24. | | |
| 25. | | |

## EAP Projects (Synthesizing) for Unit 1

| Short Assignment | Longer Assignment |
|---|---|
| **My Dream Office/Workspace** | **Social Observation Report** |
| Describe your dream work environment. What kind of job do you have? Where is it located? What is special about your office or workspace? What factors influence the design of the space? Share your ideas with a small group. | Choose a place where a lot of students spend time. Sit in a place where you can observe different greetings and examples of *I'm sorry* and *Excuse me* responses. Pay attention to tone and nonverbal cues as well. Take notes on what you hear. Prepare a report that discusses your interpretation of the interaction. Prepare to present your report to the class. Use process words and phrases in your presentation. |

## EAP Projects (Synthesizing) for Unit 2

| Short Assignment | Longer Assignment |
|---|---|
| **Compare and Contrast** | **How Should We Advise This Person?** |
| Line up so that half the class faces the other half of the class. For one minute, talk with the person across from you. Make statements comparing and contrasting what each of you like to study, eat, wear, or watch on television. You may choose other topics to compare and contrast as well. After one minute, move to the right and compare/contrast with the next person. | Look at the local newspapers or online for the advice columns. Choose a letter asking for advice that you think is interesting. Do not show the answer to anyone yet. Pass the letter around the class. Collect advice from others in the class on the same piece of paper. Then read your letter, all the advice, and then the advice the "expert" from the newspaper gave. Prepare a short presentation for your classmates. |

## Synthesizing: EAP Projects (Synthesizing) for Unit 3

| Short Assignment | Longer Assignment |
| --- | --- |
| On the Phone | My Collection |
| Write something that you would like to buy and a type of food you would like to eat on a piece of paper. For example, you may write "I'd like to buy flowers for my friend's birthday" or "I want to try Thai food." Turn in your paper. Your instructor will give you someone else's paper. Find a store or restaurant and call that business to learn more information. Include at least one piece of information that cannot be found online. Bring information about the places, locations, prices, or other details you learn from your calls. Be prepared to exchange information. | Prepare a presentation on something you collect. Talk about why you collect this item, where you get your items, and how many items are currently in your collection. Then explain how you classify the items and give examples. Bring some examples or pictures to use as visual aids for your presentation. Include phrases from Unit 3. |

## Synthesizing: EAP Projects (Synthesizing) for Unit 4

| Short Assignment | Longer Assignment |
| --- | --- |
| World Events | Current Events |
| Work with a group. Make a list of the ten events that you think are most important in world history. Rank them in order with the most important being number one. Give at least one reason why each one is on the top ten list. | As a class, make a list of current events at your school, in your city, or in the world. Then form two teams. One team will make a list of positive aspects of the events. The other team will make a list of the negative aspects. Take turns presenting your arguments to the other team. Make sure to use the best phrases when you are guessing and when you are expressing certainty. Be prepared for your classmates to interrupt if they have information to add. |

## EAP Projects (Synthesizing) for Unit 5

| Short Assignment | Longer Assignment |
|---|---|
| Where in the World? | Posters |
| Think of a location. It should be a place that your classmates are familiar with. It could be somewhere on campus, a place in the city, or a well-known city anywhere in the world. Your classmates will have a chance to ask questions as they try to guess the place you are thinking of. For example, they might say, "Is it in the U.S.?" You will have to confirm if each guess is correct or incorrect. Give your classmates 20 questions to guess correctly. | Imagine you have the chance to present a poster session at a chemistry conference. Prepare a poster. Choose an element from the periodic table. Then decide on four subtopics about the element and three details for each. Create your poster to present and describe to the rest of the class. Be prepared to answer a few questions when your classmates ask for an explanation. Give explanations and state if they are correct or incorrect as necessary. |

## EAP Projects (Synthesizing) for Unit 6

| Short Assignment | Longer Assignment |
|---|---|
| Give Me More Information | Museum Research |
| Work with a partner. Take turns naming things you see around you or know about. Ask your partner for a reaction (positive or negative). Your partner will give a reaction and two reasons for the reaction. Some things you can name include colors, restaurants, food items, pieces of art, different classes, vacation spots, sports, television shows, or movies. | Do light research on one of the Top 10 Most Visited Museums. Prepare a short presentation about the museum. Consider including details about what artists are exhibited there, famous pieces of art, and other details that may be reasons why it is a popular museum. Give your presentation to the rest of the class. |

Printed and bound by CPI Group (UK) Ltd, Croydon, CR0 4YY

13/04/2025

14656540-0001